ABANDONED SHOPPING CARTS

Personal and Spiritual Responsibility

WILLIAM BEZANSON

ABANDONED SHOPPING CARTS
Personal and Spiritual Responsibility

WILLIAM BEZANSON

Order this book online at www.trafford.com
or email orders@trafford.com

Most Trafford titles are also available at major online book retailers.

Printed in the United States of America.

ISBN: 978-1-4269-8949-0 (sc)
ISBN: 978-1-4269-8950-6 (hc)
ISBN: 978-1-4269-8951-3 (e)

Library of Congress Control Number: 2011913938

Trafford rev. 08/31/2011

 www.trafford.com

North America & international
toll-free: 1 888 232 4444 (USA & Canada)
phone: 250 383 6864 ♦ fax: 812 355 4082

By the same author:

Performance Support Solutions: Achieving Business Goals Through Enabling User Performance

Why Are Gas Prices So High? (Want a Better World? Slow Down And Save)

Making Products Obvious: Performance-Centered Design

Life of Phi: Beauty and the Golden Ratio

For Susan

In memory of my parents,
Howard and Marie Bezanson

Table of Contents

Acknowledgments

I am happy to acknowledge suggestions and comments from readers of earlier versions of this book: Nancy Berranger, Greg Bezanson, Maureen Bezanson, Melanie Chursinoff, Giovanni Lamonica, Ashley Van Sertima, Audrey Van Sertima, Frank Van Sertima, Susan Van Sertima, and George Wykoff.

I extend my thanks to Ivan Ronayne for many discussions that helped to clarify my thinking for this book; to Steve Bezanson, for giving me the cartoon about the Large Hadron Collider; to Paul Jones, for giving me the picture of the Saudi Arabian mega shopping cart; and to Gerry McDaniel, for providing information on some of the costs to his business of providing shopping carts to his customers.

The book was expertly edited by Elizabeth Tevlin. Her contribution opened up my view to be compassionate to shopping cart abandoners, to consolidate and restructure some sections, and to ponder deeply about my intentions for the book. Based on her recommendations I did considerable rewriting of the manuscript.

Any remaining errors or deficiencies in the book are due to my own neglect, not that of the editor or any of the reviewers.

This book is written in memory of my parents, Howard and Marie Bezanson, both deceased. They engendered in me a sense of responsibility on many levels, leading to my inspiration to write this book. This acknowledgment of my memory of Mom and Dad marks my gratitude, admiration, and love for them.

My lovely wife, Susan, is my dedicatee for the book. She tolerated and encouraged my research and writing, and she continues to provide the environment of love and peacefulness that I have come to treasure. This book is For Susan.

Permissions

Most of the images used in this book are pictures taken by the author (the pictures of abandoned shopping carts were not fabricated or staged; they are photographs of actual situations), or were purchased from the royalty-free service of Can Stock Photo (www.canstockphoto.com); or are in the public domain. Others, for which permission was granted, are cited on the pages in which they appear.

Prelude

Nature exists. It has always existed, and it always will exist.

It was not created. It has always existed.

Nature evolved, and it continues to evolve.

This universe came into being by means of natural processes taking place among the other universes.

Life forms always existed, they evolved, and they continue to evolve.

Nature has both physical and spiritual forms. The physical forms can be perceived and measured with physical senses and mechanisms. The spiritual forms cannot be perceived with physical senses, but require spiritual senses to do so.

Space and time do not exist. Everything is happening *Here, Now*!

Introduction

One sees abandoned shopping carts everywhere, especially in the parking lots of shopping centres and grocery stores. This one was placed up on a concrete median, thus showing a bit of consideration on the part of its abandoner by not leaving it in the way of cars or pedestrians.

At one time the earth was a big place, so big that its size was inconceivable to humans. It was even considered to be flat. One's actions had essentially no impact on the planet.

Now, in modern times, the earth is a small place. It is now undeniably spherical, and its former huge 8,000 mile diameter is now not quite a mere 13,000 km. Our perceptions of size have changed. Television news brings the most distant conflict, earthquake, and famine right into our homes with live coverage.

The earth has become so small, in many people's conception of it, that we can easily see all of it, examine all of it, and think about all of it. Nobody else of significance will do our thinking for us. We must think for ourselves about our relationship with the earth. We must not make an abandoned shopping cart of our Home.

Where else can we go if we ruin our home? Who else will help us if we let the earth rot to the point of not being able to sustain human life? How can we survive, even with super-advanced technology, when there is nowhere to exist in living form? Why would we allow such a situation to manifest?

But life can be so busy for us that we hardly have time to realize how the earth has shrunk, in our reality, but of course not in actuality. Our activities have grown tremendously. Virtually every interaction that we have has increased somehow, in complexity, in number, in frequency, and in other ways. There are more items to read, more demands on time, more things to buy, more trips to take, more electronic-based social network interactions, more health concerns, more financial options, and so on. Who has time to think about our impacts on the planet, and to do anything about them?

But think we must!

Nobody else will think for us. In fact, many organizations depend on us *not* to think. Marketers don't want us to think, but to keep buying. Bankers don't want us to think, but to keep borrowing. Religious leaders don't want us to think, but to keep being faithful sheep. Governments don't want us to think, but to keep paying taxes and voting to reelect the politicians. Medical practitioners don't want us to think, but to keep taking pills in compliance with directions from their real masters: the pharmaceutical companies. Teachers don't want us to think, but to memorize, regurgitate, and graduate. Parents don't want us to think, but to be like them. The list goes on and on.

The prime goal of thinking is to make rational judgments. And the most vital issue for which we must make some rational judgments is concerning the fragility of our delicately balanced, precious, island home, the Earth.

We must think for ourselves, so that we can make right choices! This is the only reasonable course of action for us. In short, we must all be personally responsible for the earth's environment, its sustainability, and its future ... and also for humanity's evolution, sustainability, and future.

Ultimately, thinking for ourselves should inspire us to do the proper actions in all circumstances, for our own lives, for the world, and for God. So this book is about not only thinking for yourself, but also doing the right thing.

I have chosen the theme of Abandoned Shopping Carts as a common thread and foundation for the chapters and articles of this book. That theme will guide us on a journey from personal responsibility, through civic responsibility, and others, to spiritual responsibility. Each chapter is divided into a set of articles. Through each article the fundamental question about the topic is whether we abandon it, as we might abandon a shopping cart. Or will we accept our responsibility to take care of the world, ourselves, our communities, and so on?

In the first chapter, we start by looking at some pictures of shopping carts that have been abandoned, and think about what motivated the people who abandoned them. We then look at other forms of littering and neglect of our earth's environment in Chapter 2. The next chapter broadens our scope to examine several aspects of responsibility to our communities and countries.

Chapter 4 considers our personal responsibility to our selves, including proper thinking, thriftiness, decision making, and other topics. Then, in the next chapter, we address the topic of responsible dealings with other people, such as our customers, family, and friends. Finally, Chapter 6 considers the most important topic of all, namely spiritual responsibility. By being fully responsible to our spiritual selves, all else follows. With mature spirituality, we automatically adopt a sincere responsibility for all the other topics that are covered in this book.

An interlude mid-way through the book and a postlude at the end give a fictional account of mankind's evolution from the lofty perspective of spiritual beings entrusted with the responsibility of inspiring us to self-preservation and growth.

To give you a sense of the overall flavour of the book, let's consider what is your mission or purpose in life. What do you hope to accomplish before you die? Why were you born here, now, in this form?

Just as a lighthouse gives ships a guide, a directional indicator, and a warning of danger, so a well-defined mission and purpose for your life provide guidance, indicators, and warnings as you navigate the various calm and rough seas of your life.

I have no idea what your mission is, but I do very much recommend that you formulate it.

The best I can do, perhaps, is to explain what my own mission is. My hope is that by doing so, I might inspire you to strive to find your own. The lighthouse for your Life can be encapsulated into a well-researched statement of your mission. That's why working on such a statement is important.

For many years I wandered around in mission-land, bouncing from one inspiration to another. I was attracted to numerous noble ideals, and read about one or more for a time, then switched to another. I admired people who seemed to know their purpose in life, and who focused their work and energies on achieving that purpose. I tried to emulate them, felt guilty when I fell short, and wallowed in a sense of inadequacy when I could not live up to the achievements of a Gandhi, or an Einstein, or a Trump.

Finally, later in life, various influences drew me toward the notion of *service* as a core concept in my mission. These influences included some Jungian Analysis, mystical studies, comparative religion studies, and others. After some iteration in the wording, I eventually formulated my mission to be:

Help to bring about a spiritual state in this mundane world.

That is now my mission in life, my purpose in being here. I now believe that this statement summarizes why I was born here, in this body, at this time.

This physical world indeed is very mundane. Overall it is secular and people have lost sight of higher ideals. Mankind has grown self-centered and lazy; we have forgotten where we came from, where we are going, and how we are sustained. We are destroying the earth through over stretching its resources, through polluting them, and through lack of proper stewardship. Most importantly of all, we are destroying our selves, again through poor stewardship.

And our decay is illustrated in abandoning our shopping carts. Such a simple device lets us act out our inner lack of a spiritual purpose in a seemingly harmless manner, much like random acts of vandalism or graffiti on public walls. What appears to be a seemingly harmless lack of responsibility is actually the tip of the iceberg when contrasted with abandoning the spiritual purpose of our lives.

I have evolved my thinking to formulate the above mission to help bring about a better balance between the mundane and the spiritual. The Churches have had a crack at it, but have failed because they only teach religion. Jungian psychology has had a try, but it reaches far too small an audience. Many authors have attempted, but people are too distracted to pay attention and to change fundamentally.

Do I have a chance to make a fundamental change? Can I succeed where the Churches and Jungians and famous authors have failed? I don't know, but I'm determined to try.

Nothing is more urgent, to my way of thinking, for saving humanity and the world as regaining a balance between the spiritual and the mundane. Our spiritual lives are greatly in need of focus and development.

So that gives you an idea of the mission that I have developed for my life. My hope is that you will examine your own life deeply and work on developing—or discovering, or realizing, or formulating—a goal, a mission, a purpose for your life.

My further hope is that this book will help you in that task. Ultimately, I hope that it will contribute to raising people's consciousness to a higher level of accepting responsibility for their actions and impacts on humanity and the world. Writing this book is in support of my mission. If it prompts even a few readers to grow in personal and spiritual responsibility, and to spread the word, then my mission will be incrementally successful.

I want to make it clear that I do not expect you to agree with my views that I present here. Moreover, I do not want you blindly to change your way of thinking over to my own way. What I do want is for you to think for yourself about each of the issues that I raise, and then to do the right thing, however it is that you interpret what is right. My own views are explained here only as examples of how I view the world, examples for you to consider, to research, and to ponder. But you must make up your own mind.

My views may be controversial, and I accept the risk of revealing them publically. For example, I expect that you may not agree with some of my ideas about civic responsibility, or about how to make decisions, or about my conception of God and how to pray, but I do want you to read them as examples to consider, and then to decide for yourself.

This book presents a personal view, to stimulate your thinking. I am not acting on behalf of any organization. My only agenda is saving humanity and the world.

For conciseness in the book, I often use masculine pronouns and adjectives, such as "he" and "him", to designate both masculine and feminine, such as "his or her".

This book is a logical extension of my earlier book *Why Are Gas Prices so High?*, which I recommend reading in conjunction with it.

This book was motivated by prayer; therefore it cannot fail to achieve its purpose. (See "How to Pray" on page 179.)

Chapter 1: Abandoned shopping carts

Here we see a couple of carts abandoned at the edge of a grocery store parking lot, just as a pathway starts. It would appear that people wheel their groceries to the pathway and then carry them from there, leaving the carts behind. The pathway leading to an apartment building in the distance gives us a clue to where some of the abandoners might live.

For years I have been annoyed to see shopping carts abandoned in parking lots, roadside ditches, and elsewhere.

I was also annoyed to see how many people had adopted an attitude of uncaring relinquishment of personal responsibility in many areas of life, such as littering, driving rudely, not voting in elections, and so on.

Was there a connection between these two annoyances?

Eventually I came to see abandoned shopping carts as a remarkably vivid symbol of modern society's abandonment of individual responsibility. Many people shrug and think "Not my job! Somebody else will do it! I'm too busy! Why should I care?"

Seeing a shopping cart carelessly left aside, especially away from its rightful property and tipped over, can be a sad sight. There seems to be a story there. What was the cart's user thinking? Does the user feel guilty? Did bystanders care? Did they intervene? How can people be so lazy and irresponsible? If shopping carts had feelings, how would they feel to be abandoned? What is the additional price on my grocery bill that reflects the charges incurred by the grocery store owner, who has to fetch those abandoned carts and replace the ones that are damaged or lost?

Note that in the e-commerce business (Internet-based buying and selling) the online mechanism of "shopping cart" is an accepted practice of gathering items for purchase during a "checkout" phase of a transaction. Interestingly, there is a marketing problem called "abandoned shopping carts" whereby customers add items to their virtual, online shopping carts and then abandon them, disconnecting from the transaction before completing it. It is not my intent to elaborate on the topic of online shopping cart abandonment in this book, other than mentioning it here in order to illustrate how the social acceptance of irresponsibility can influence even our online behaviour.

From a sociological viewpoint, irresponsibility is contagious and possibly even encouraged in subtle ways, as we might infer from this picture. Indeed, the really serious impact of such irresponsibility is a social one: that which gets abandoned goes well beyond mere shopping carts, to include common sense, decency, thriftiness, civility, spirituality, and more.

This first chapter focuses on the literal abandonment of physical shopping carts and on some of their interesting stories. In subsequent chapters we will see how such abandonment reflects a decline of personal responsibility in society.

Shopping cart by a bus stop

Bus stops provide one of the most frequent abandoning grounds for shopping carts. One of their regular postures is tipped over. How traumatic! It's one insult to be abandoned, but much more hurtful to be tipped over as well.

This picture shows a shopping cart tipped over beside a bus stop on a suburban street in Ottawa, Canada, where I live. I watched it for several days as I drove past it. At first it had been simply left on the grass beside the bus stop. After a day or so, I saw that it had been tipped over. Another couple of days passed, and still nobody had removed the cart. So eventually I took this picture.

What is its story? Perhaps some bus-commuting shopper wheeled it from the store to the bus stop (a long distance in this case, perhaps a five- or ten-minute walk) and left it there when the bus arrived. Did anyone raise an objection to that shopper? Did the bus driver reprimand him or her? Did any bus passenger or bystander speak up? Did the shopper feel guilty, either on abandoning the cart or at any time afterwards on seeing the poor cart tipped over when passing that scene of the crime?

My guess is "No" to all of the above questions. Everyone looked the other way. They figured that it was not their job to correct the shopper or to take back the cart to its proper place. And, no, the original offender perhaps felt no guilt, because he learned from the isolationism of modern society that he was quite entitled to behave that way.

And, I have to admit, I did not move the cart back to its rightful place; I just took its picture.

As I ponder that admission of mine, I can feel a subtle attunement with shopping cart abandoners. Perhaps they were too busy to return their carts, just as I was too busy to interrupt my driving to make the effort to wheel this cart by the bus stop all the way back to where it belonged. Besides, where would I leave my car while performing this good deed? Would I look silly, pushing an empty cart down the road? Maybe I would get a parking ticket for deserting my car while returning the cart. Maybe I'll be late for my appointment.

Yes, attunement is right! Every abandoner likely has his own reasons for doing what they do to shopping carts. Perhaps he was in a desperate hurry, or was angry about having to take the cart back to its corral, or just mad at his lot in life and took it out on the cart. There must be a lot of angry people in the world, judging by the number of deserted carts that I see all around.

What strange thoughts and emotions one must be experiencing, not only to abandon a shopping cart, shirking one's responsibility, but also to tip it over, like some piece of junk?

Of course, there might be other reasons that a cart is tipped over. Perhaps it was initially standing upright (merely abandoned) and a later bypasser tipped it over (an accomplice abandoner). Or a wheel might have been broken, causing it to tip. Or maybe the wind blew it over. That's it! Spread the guilt around . . . anything to make people feel better.

Shopping cart dumping ground

Abandoned shopping carts attract other abandoned shopping carts. Either that, or they give birth to others of their kind overnight!

Here's a wonderful illustration of unreasonable crowd behaviour: sheep following sheep. This pile of shopping carts is just on the periphery of the parking lot of a grocery store not far from where I live. Somebody pushed a cart to that spot some time ago, rather than taking a few extra steps to the shopping cart corral. Somebody else added his cart to the same area. Then someone else …. Soon many people assumed that it was an acceptable place to toss their carts.

I expect that every single one of those people, if asked, would admit that the haphazard pile of carts was not the official drop off place for them. They would agree that a few extra steps for them would not hurt. But, like sheep, they simply followed the crowd and shrugged.

Shopping cart left in a hallway

This cart must feel either very lonely or very proud to be at a unique location.

Now here's a blatant one! I could not believe it!

On a visit to an apartment building, I was astonished to see a shopping cart abandoned in a hallway. My first hope was that someone had left it in the hall temporarily, while unpacking a load, and that within minutes they would return the cart all the way back to the grocery store or wherever it belonged. I made a mental note to check whether the cart would be removed when I finished my visit, perhaps an hour or so later.

But, No! The cart was still there. Wow! That one was worth a picture!

If the cart was left outside the door of the offender, then that person seems to have had no qualms about advertising his irresponsibility. If, on the other hand, someone had wheeled the cart along the hall and left it outside someone else's door, then what a cowardly thing to do! Will we ever know the full story? Only the cart knows.

Cart on a suburban street

Do you suppose that someone might have interpreted these diagonal stripes, delineated by a curved line, as a designated place to abandon shopping carts?

This one is blatant, subtle, and shameful.

It is blatant because someone deliberately abandoned this shopping cart out on the street, by the curb, away from any houses. Presumably, that person was hoping to remain anonymous. It is likely not far from the offender's house; otherwise he would have had to wheel it some distance down the street before leaving it, rather than just pushing it out after dark when being seen was unlikely. What must that person think every day, when he looks out his window or walks out from his front door, and sees the cart that he put there? Does he feel any pangs of guilt? Does he feel annoyed that "someone" has not removed the cart yet? Does he feel any embarrassment? Maybe because it is not *directly* in front of his house, he can forget about it and perhaps even convince himself that someone else had put it there.

On the other hand, it is subtle, because being on city property, rather than on some private property, it would appear to have been abandoned there by that ubiquitous Someone Else, that Other Person, Not Me.

And, finally, it is shameful. The fact that it remained there, on the street for more than a week shames every one of us, myself included, who drove or walked by and did nothing about the cart. Every few days I found it moved a few metres this way or that way, and even up on the lawn around the corner. So clearly somebody felt the urge to clean up the street a bit, shuffling garbage around a bit, but resisted the urge (and embarrassment) to go to the trouble to take the cart all the way back to its rightful place. That's somebody else's job!

Beside a corral

FIRST PRIZE: Laziness and irresponsibility highlighted!

Can you believe this?

Here is a cart abandoned right beside a corral!

I can understand someone abandoning a shopping cart way out there, a long walk from the nearest shopping cart corral. Maybe they were in a hurry; maybe the kids were crying in the car; maybe they had recently received some very bad news.

But *beside the corral*? How irresponsible can one get? How self-centered and inconsiderate!

Just three or four extra steps!

To be generous, I have to admit that the person at least left the cart in the general vicinity of the corral, thereby lessening the work that somebody else must do to clean up. However, even this generosity gets overruled when you consider that the abandoned cart effectively blocks a parking spot, and thus annoys and inconveniences numerous people who might get their hopes up on spotting a blank spot in the row of cars, only to have their hopes dashed on closer inspection.

This one takes the prize!

A look at shopping cart economics

Does anyone ever consider, when "borrowing" and abandoning a shopping cart, what it costs for the cart owner, who runs a business, perhaps a grocery store or a drug store, to search for, retrieve, transport, repair, and otherwise clean up after such vandalism? For sure, those costs get factored into the cost of doing business, so we all pay for them. Thus we all have an interest in changing shopping cart abandoners into shopping cart stewards.

Being interested in what goes on behind the scenes, I wanted to know something about what it costs to look after abandoned shopping carts. So I talked with Gerry McDaniel, the owner of my local grocery store, and learned a lot.

A typical shopping cart, I learned, costs about $200 (Canadian funds). One can spend much more, for high-end ones, with electronically-locking wheels at the periphery of the store's property, for example, say $300 or more. And similarly, a stripped-down model might cost less than $150. But $200 is typical for a good, general-purpose, medium-sized model.

Over a cart's lifetime, an owner or manager might pay for maintenance, due to damage or breakage, in the same range as for the initial cost, thus doubling the cost. Thus a $200 cart might cost around $400 over its life cycle, plus labour of various sorts.

A store owner or manager has to deal with carts that are "borrowed" and abandoned. Either one of the store staff has to drive around and retrieve such carts, or a separate contractor must be hired for such a function. A typical charge for a contractor is in the range of three dollars per retrieved cart, or perhaps a flat fee of, say $15 per day. For Gerry's inventory of about 175 shopping carts, some 20 to 25 carts go missing each week, and need retrieval. He has had to buy 50 to 75 carts each year to keep his inventory well stocked. You can do the math to see something of this cost of running the business.

Shopping carts are sometimes "borrowed" for other uses, other than for carting away the groceries. One sees such carts in strange places, such as apartment buildings, for the convenience of residents for various purposes. An extreme example, cited by Gerry, had to do with a family holiday. He arrived at his store early to find the entire stock of shopping carts missing! It turned out that families had used his store parking lot to leave their cars, they had taken carts to wheel the children to the celebrations, and they had mostly not returned the carts but abandoned them at the site of the festivities. Guess who had to pay for the retrieval of all those carts.

Who would have thought that running a business would involve such logistics and costs as accommodating the inconsiderate folk who borrow and abandon shopping carts?

On the other hand, let's consider a more compassionate view of a shopping cart abandoner's motivation. Many of the carts are left at the edge of a parking lot or near a bus stop. That pattern suggests that those abandoners did not drive cars, but took the bus or walked home, carrying their purchases. But shopping cart corrals are typically in the midst of parking lots, at places that are inconvenient for such shoppers. So, it would seem that shopping carts are mostly intended for car drivers, and that the needs of pedestrians and bus riders are not considered. This situation would suggest that additional shopping cart corrals might thoughtfully be placed at the edge of the store's property, leading to a bus stop or to a frequently travelled pedestrian route.

Looking at the behaviour of shopping cart abandoners in this new light opens up the idea that they are not being neglectful or irresponsible, but simply living their lives in a different manner than we might have expected. Maybe they are unconsciously starting a grass-roots movement that allows people to behave in natural ways, thereby urging systems such as shopping cart protocols to adapt to human styles, rather than forcing humans to adapt to systems, as has historically been the case.

Addressing the needs of non-driving shopping cart users reminds me of a natural method of designing pathways and roadways: follow the paths that cows choose to come home at night, rather than laying out roads with right angles, straight lines, and so on. Humans have their own style; design for them. Observe every deviation from "proper" behaviour, such as grass-trodden shortcuts joining straight-lined concrete walkways, as not a problem, but an opportunity—an indication of how to enhance a design to accommodate real needs.

Now, this suggestion of new, peripheral corrals adds further to the economic challenges of store owners. But I'll bet that a business case could be developed that shows the long-term financial advantage of accommodating shoppers who do not drive cars, if we consider the good will that it will attract, the subtle incentive not to drive cars and thereby reduce pollution and enhance our health through exercise, and increased business through addressing this and other aspects of the overall usage of non-car driving shoppers. Besides, it's nicer than ignoring them.

Chapter 2: Destroying the earth's environment

One of the chief causes of the degradation of the earth's environment is our overconsumption of consumer goods. This mega shopping cart, a marketing gimick at an Al Khobar, Saudi Arabia shopping mall, symbolizes overconsumption beautifully! If everybody filled up shopping carts of that size, the earth would be in more trouble than we could handle! (Either that, or it is the Cart of the Titans, who shop there regularly.)

This chapter addresses broader topics than just abandoned shopping carts, such as littering, cleaning up after oneself, overconsumption, and other acts of irresponsibility. The overall issue is still similar: shrugging with a "don't care" attitude and assuming that someone else will clean up or pay the penalty.

Now we are told that even drinking bottled water deteriorates the planet, depleting petroleum to make the plastic, polluting the atmosphere by manufacturing and transporting the bottles, and junking up the environment with billions of discarded plastic bottles—not to mention poisoning our bodies with chemicals that leach from the plastic.

Littering: Throwing out a stove in a parking lot

Shopping carts aren't the only thing that get abandoned. Brains also get abandoned.

Guess how astonished I was to see this thrown-out, broken-down stove in a shopping centre parking lot. Occasionally one sees a stove left at the end of someone's driveway for garbage pickup; but in a parking lot? That's what I would call super-littering, or perhaps hyper-littering!

The story is deeper than it might appear on the surface. That specific spot in that shopping centre parking lot was used for many years as a drop-off depot for a clothing charity group, with a few well marked bins for putting bags of clothing and small household items into. Suddenly the bins were missing. Presumably the agency that collected and distributed the items decided to stop using that location. But the public memory persisted. Somebody seems to have grown accustomed to using that location as a dumping ground for not just small, soft items, but also for big, hard ones. Irresponsibility triumphed! The stove found a new junkyard! Try to imagine what was going though the mind of the person who left the stove there? Did he feel any guilt? Did he have any caring for the person who must clean up afterwards? Will he return and clean up his own mess? Will he dump again?

Charitable drop-off sites provide a good service, enabling us to dispose of things we don't need any longer, and benefitting the agencies and people who could use them. What I'm really pointing out here is the lack of common sense that some people can exhibit through unthinking littering.

Leave each campsite cleaner than you found it

The number of people who mess up a beautiful camping area such as this one should grow smaller each year, eventually reaching zero.

When I was a Boy Scout several decades ago I was taught the ethical principle "Leave each campsite cleaner than you found it!"

Since that time, essentially all of my adult life, I have tried to follow that principle, to set a good example for others, to teach our children to respect our beautiful world, and to do my best to clean up after myself.

Of course, the principle applies not only to campsites but also to every location that one touches. It is easy to clean the "campsite" many times per day: don't litter, wipe down the counter in public washrooms after using them, move dirty dishes to the sink after eating, and by numerous other little methods.

It is astonishing to observe just how very many people seem to have adopted the opposite creed: "Leave each campsite dirtier than you found it!" Who do they think will clean up after them? Their mothers?

If each of us could do only one thing consistently to develop our sense of personal responsibility, I would vote for this one: "Leave each campsite cleaner than you found it!" It is such a simple and effective way to start. And then the habit will likely grow to include other types of responsibility.

This maxim, once it becomes a habit, is very powerful. Each of us can clean up after ourselves, and after others. Each of us can teach others, through our example, to take care of our world. Each of us can be stewards of not only our own little worlds, but also of the whole World!

Resist overconsumption

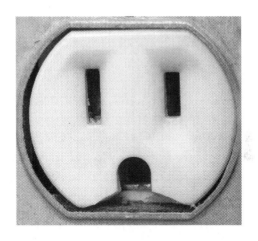

An electrical outlet symbolizes overconsumption beautifully. I'd like to see each of us minimize our usage of electricity. I love this particular picture. It looks like a stylized mini-face, gasping in horror, from deep in electricity-land, at how much energy we overconsume and waste.

Overconsumption in Western society has been rampant for years. Sometimes you have to step outside of your normal life for a while, for example, travel to a foreign country, especially if you work there or stay there for a significant time, in order to appreciate, on your return home, just how much we have in our developed world. Nearly everyone I talk with after they return from such a trip resolves to cut back, slow down, or declutter their lives.

And overconsumption is not new. It has been going on for decades. At least that is the case in my country, Canada, since the 1950s or '60s.

I think that this behaviour stems from a distortion of capitalism. Originally business enterprises tried to determine what customers needed, and they created products to fulfill that need. Capitalism became hugely successful in doing that: satisfying people's needs.

This model of the economy worked well throughout the twentieth century, up until about the 1960s, when, to a large extent, people found that their needs had become fulfilled. They had two cars in the family, a nice home, a dishwasher, and other marks of success, and they did not need much more. The marketing folk realized that people would soon stop buying new products, because their basic needs were fulfilled.

So the marketers convinced their companies to move from satisfying basic needs to creating new needs. Since the late 1960s, companies started to build obsolescence into products, so that people would want (not need) to buy the next version. Each new generation of products was "new and improved", and customers lined up to buy them. New needs soon appeared, which we never even realized that we had. Think of mouthwash and deodorants; videotapes, then videodisks, then DVDs, and most recently BluRay systems; minivans, then SUVs; three or more generations of cell phones; digital cameras; ever faster and more powerful personal computers; and the list goes on.

Those marketers aimed at younger and younger children to plant the idea that they needed to buy more and more products, to grow up to be good consumers. They have even focused on convincing adults to be like children, building products to let us play games, to amuse ourselves, to be distracted from our adult responsibilities.

And here we are, with a global financial crisis and debt (at the time of writing, 2008-09), stemming from overconsumption and from confusing wants with needs.

So, how can we break out of this vicious, self-regenerating crisis? Simple! We can consume less; we can buy less; we can voluntarily cut back our lifestyles a bit. Each of us in the developed world can cut back a bit, say ten or fifteen percent, without suffering much; and if a huge number of us did so, we would make an enormous contribution to restoring our economy to a healthy state. Moreover, it is a moral approach. Not cutting back might be considered immoral. Finally, doing so would revive our sense of personal responsibility, thereby making us more human and helping to advance the evolution of mankind. Not doing so will likely lead to irreparable harm to this experiment with Life on this, our island home that we call Earth.

More fundamentally, we can think for ourselves. We can observe what is happening in the world, analyze what we see, and conclude whether we want the situation to remain. We don't have to wait for governments to mandate lifestyle changes through taxes, tariffs, penalties, incentives, and rules. They only think ahead as far as the next election.

But we can all think ahead much, much farther than that! In order to save the world for future generations we, every one of us, must think for ourselves. We must realize that only we can change ourselves. And only we can save the world. We must elevate our sense of responsibility to see the Big Picture.

Slow down. Buy less. Think more. Consume less. Act responsibly!

Why are gas prices so high? Drive the speed limit.

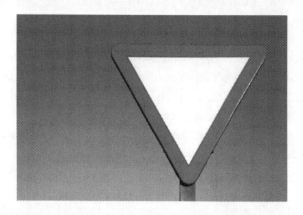

This is the standard traffic sign in much of the world for Give Way, for yielding to other traffic, for slowing down, for being cautious.

"Why are gas prices so high?" Joe was moaning, grumbling about his pet peeve.

"Because you pay those prices," responded Claire. She and Joe were chatting downtown, at one of their regular lunch meetings.

"Huh? Of course I pay the prices—that's what it costs!"

"No, it's not like that," explained Claire. "Price has nothing to do with cost. If I had a bucket full of gas, and I wanted to sell some of it to you, and you wanted to buy it from me, we would negotiate a price that we would both be content with."

Joe agreed, "Well ... OK!"

"And if you didn't like my price, you could simply leave and shop elsewhere, perhaps at my neighbour's."

"But suppose your neighbour charged the same price?"

"Then you would have three choices, wouldn't you? First, you could give up and pay that price. Second, you could set up your own gas business and charge people what you like. And third, you could reduce your gas consumption."

Joe thought for a moment, and said, "Yeah! Pay their price! That's what we do all the time! ... Uh! ... How would reducing my consumption make any difference to the price of gas?"

"Well," began Claire, "if you bought less of my gas, I would reduce its price."

"Huh?" This strange logic surprised Joe.

Claire continued. "I would charge less, because I would be stuck with an inventory of gas, and a lower price would encourage my customers to buy it.

"And you can easily use less gas by driving more slowly," she explained. Her inspiration was leading her along now. She felt excited. "Suppose that you slowed down and drove at or slightly below the speed limit all of the time. My guess is that you would then be driving, say, 15 or 20% slower than you do now. So, to a first approximation, you would use about 15 or 20% less gas, and maybe even more. That could amount to a savings of around $250 to $500 per year for a typical driver. Now, if everyone drove at the speed limit, think of the pressure that would put on the gas companies! Prices would drop dramatically! We could change the world!"

. . .

Claire and Joe were talking again, a year later. "It's hard to believe what happened," Joe started. "I never would have guessed that so many people would catch on so quickly to your suggestion!"

"I guess the mood was right for it to spread," admitted Claire, modestly.

"Right on!" Joe was enthusiastic. "Shortly after I started driving at the speed limit I started to feel more relaxed. And that pleasant mood flowed over into other aspects of my life. I looked around and saw the trees. I could even 'take time to smell the flowers', as the old maxim goes. I became more peaceful and patient, and found that I really didn't need to drive so many places after all. I had more time to help my children with their homework, and I became more attentive to my wife. It's amazing how it all clicked!"

"Yes, and as you know from the news reports," Claire added, "You're not the only one. Evidently people all over the world were ready to make such a change. It's like the time was right, somehow, for the 'speed limit' movement to spread like wildfire."

Joe agreed, "And can you believe the result? People are more peaceful, and more civil to each other. Prices for all sorts of things are down. Fewer accidents, sales of large vehicles are dropping, insurance prices will soon be way down. Less exhaust emission, causing less pollution ...."

Claire was hopeful that the trend would continue. "Well, we can be proud that we might have started something, or at least that we were there at the start. It's like the old adage of thinking globally, but acting locally. We have perhaps helped to save the world, and humanity, by simply driving at the speed limit!"[1]

---

1   Adapted from W. Bezanson, *Why Are Gas Prices So High?—Want a Better World: Slow Down and Save*, Bloomington, IN: Trafford

The large hadron collider

The Large Hadron Collider is fascinating to me. Most modern physics concepts are fascinating to me, and this system aims to explore the most fundamental concepts of all, so it is perhaps the most fascinating. It has the potential to do massive damage, because it tampers with elementary forces, but it also should be able to help us to understand the universe.[2]

The Large Hadron Collider (LHC) deep underground in Switzerland and France is perhaps the biggest scientific experimental tool ever developed. The plan is that it will generate such enormous energy in accelerating sub-atomic particles to bash into each other at nearly the speed of light that particles at an even more fundamental level will materialize, including the Higgs Boson (the "God Particle"), for studying

---

Publishing, 2006.

2   Cartoon taken from ffffound.com/image/106aa08ac6baacd96179802 271ab9f809baed135?c=1565323 and used by permission.

conditions similar to those of the Big Bang, when our universe came into being, about 13.7 billion years ago. Some physicists have cautioned that mini-black holes might also materialize, and if they get out of control, they could grow and swallow us all up, and perhaps even annihilate our solar system, if not more. Other scientists call those guys fear mongers, and assure us that there is no need to worry.

The LHC was supposed to come online in 2007, but its launch has been delayed several times due to a construction accident in 2005 and flaws with peripheral subsystems, such as the superconducting magnets and vacuum systems in 2008 and 2009. It is still not fully operational as of November 2009.

Let me speculate for a bit, about how our future might unfold:

At some future time, say a few centuries from now, some physicists are sitting around chatting and watching their time viewer as an idle pastime. They see mankind in our era, say around 2007, developing an LHC, and they know for sure that if it ever gets fully operational it will certainly annihilate the universe. Since they exist, the physicists conclude that the LHC never did get up and running, so they realize that they have a responsibility to go back in time to sabotage the LHC. They do just that, and introduce all sorts of bugs into the magnetic accelerators, the cooling system, and so on. The LHC gets abandoned, and the physicists break out the champagne, with great relief.

Is that the way we will let the future unfold? Will we neglect our earth's development and our own future, to the point that we will depend on our smart descendents to develop the technology to look back on us and to come back to save us? Are we really that irresponsible?

I have no idea whether the LHC will annihilate the universe, or whether it is the greatest tool ever invented. I am not such a Luddite that I curse every new tool that can help mankind. Indeed, as an engineer, I applaud the development of new technology, provided that it is safe and used prudently. And I am hopeful that the LHC will be a tool that helps mankind to develop fundamental understanding and to evolve well.

But I do know that we must not depend on anyone else to save us and our planet. We must think for ourselves, protect the earth's environment, and take personal responsibility for our future. We must not be like the aliens in the above cartoon and "see what happens".

What can I do?

Our precious island home, the Earth, has sustained and nurtured us for a very long time. Now it is our turn to recognize our immense responsibility to care for and sustain our Home, and to act on that responsibility.

What can any individual person do, when facing the enormous challenges of the earth's environmental degradation?

We can shrug our shoulders. Or we can take action. We can curse the darkness, or we can light a candle.

On many occasions I have heard people moan and complain about some undesirable situation, but they do nothing about it. People complain about violence in some sports, but they don't advocate for change by contacting the relevant authorities. People are critical of community or church leaders, but they don't speak directly to those leaders to explain their point of view. People worry about what's happening to the Earth's environment, but they don't write letters to politicians arguing for more rational, long-term policies for ecological sustainability.

Such people are just shrugging their shoulders, assuming that someone else will take up the cause. Or they vote with their feet, leaving behind the messy situation by changing where they live, or what organization they belong to, or which institution they want to be part of. They drop out. They abandon their shopping carts.

But the responsible thing to do is to take action. And the biggest problem of all, the most pressing need for action, is for our world's future ability to support mankind's existence.

It used to be that the world was so big, and we were so small, that our impact on it was negligible. We could destroy trees, pollute rivers, and mess up the atmosphere with impunity. Not only were our actions so insignificant, but also our level of intelligence and knowledge were incapable of grasping the significance of our neglect.

But now we are more mature as a society, more evolved, and more knowledgeable about the world's state. And we are more numerous and more powerful, and we have magnificent machines that greatly amplify our individual efforts, thus creating more havoc and wreaking more damage than ever historically.

There are at least two fundamental reasons that we must act to protect the Earth: because we will be back, and because it is the right thing to do.

The first reason has to do with the widely-held belief that each one of us will reincarnate many times in the future, and this Earth is the only home in the universe that we know about that is suitable for mankind's needs. So, it is important to preserve the integrity of Earth's life-supporting environment not only for our children and grandchildren, but also for ourselves when we return to live here in future incarnations. Do you want nice or nasty living conditions to return to? It's your choice.

The second reason for acting to protect the Earth is because it is the right thing to do: morally, humanely, and spiritually. Stop shrugging. Just do it! (as the Nike advertising slogan used to exhort).

So, "What can I do?" you might ask. I urge you to figure that out for yourself. Do what you are uniquely capable of doing, what you came here on Earth to do, what nobody else can do as well as you can. As a grown up, mature, and evolved person, there are no excuses any more. Your parents, teachers, clergy, politicians, managers, friends, family—indeed, everyone—they all give wrong advice. They may not do so in order deliberately to mislead you. They simply don't know you optimally. They give advice not to you, but to their image of you. So stop listening and following, and start thinking and creating. And then do the right thing.

In my own case, I have chosen to write books and letters, and to give lectures on my views of how we should behave. I am not comfortable marching in public demonstrations, but I do feel good about writing and advocating my ideas to appropriate people in authority. That's also why I wrote this book and my earlier one, *Why Are Gas Prices So High?*

In your case, I urge you to find your own path. "Eat, Pray, Love", as the title of a popular book and movie states. Yes, eat of the spiritual food that is presented to you by the circumstances of your life, pray about what you see and what you can do about it, and live your life optimally and with passion and love for what you feel inwardly is right.

Chapter 3: Lack of civic responsibility

This shopping cart has a story to tell. One can almost guess what happened. That's a bus stop in the background. What you can't see is a shopping centre behind the camera. The shopper likely wheeled his purchases along the sidewalk to the bus stop, unloaded them, pushed the cart some distance off onto the lawn, and then took the bus.

We all belong to the world, to our country, to our community. With that in mind, we all have a responsibility to care for the world, our country, and so on. "We are the World!" was the anthem that the enthusiastic crowds sang at the mid-1980s "USA for Africa" fundraising events. The anthem dropped away, but the sentiment lingers. Yes, we are, indeed, the World. We don't just belong to it—we are it!

Have you ever stopped to think *What is the world?* The *earth* is easy to see, to feel, and to define. It is a physical object, and it is obvious to us all. But what is the *world*?

We are!

This concept is similar to the question "What is a church?" Most people point to a church building in response to such a question. But, as modern thinking clarifies, the church is actually the people who belong to a specific parish or congregation. We are the church. Similarly, we are the world.

That identity—we and the world—brings with it a responsibility, a civic responsibility. That is the subject of this chapter.

Responsibility in the workplace

I have always thought that the best visual representation for Human Resources in modern workplaces was an impersonal image of people holding hands. This figure of cut-out people does the trick. I would also like to see such departments mostly eliminated, as symbolized by the shadows that they cast here.

When I first heard the term Human Resources (HR) in a company back in the late 1970s, I was shocked. I had been accustomed to the term Personnel to designate the department that addressed such issues as hiring, benefits, and vacations. But the HR designation seemed so pompous, so stilted, and so inappropriate!

And I still feel that way. Nowadays, most organizations have HR functions. And while their activities and mandates have expanded over the years, I have observed HR staff members become more insular, more unclear of their role in empowering personnel, and more mistaken in the belief that they have an important role to play.

I wonder if the name change from Personnel to Human Resources has inflated the egos of the staff members of those departments, causing them to lose their proper focus. Such inflation might especially be the case for those who lived through the transition in names, say in the 1970s and '80s.

I think that such groups should return to being called the Personnel Department, or perhaps the Human Beings Department, or even the People Empowerment Department.

This preference of mine may seem trite; but I view it as profound. It is very easy to lose focus when in a group of people who think alike, who recruit people in their own image, who eat and socialize together, and who are often centrally located, removed from the people whom they serve and who provide the actual reason that the organization exists. It is very easy for such people, excellent though each individual person might be, to forget their true roles for the organization. Instead, they might develop a view that preserves their own culture, and then begin to resent their primary clients and to degrade their service to them. They might often forget that they have staff functions, not line functions; that is, they are in support roles, not contributors to the core purpose of an enterprise.

Let me explain a related situation. I first became aware of the notion of "quality control" in one of my early full time jobs at Hewlett-Packard, a huge, well-respected international electronics product manufacturer. It had a Quality Assurance department. (Other companies used the terms Quality Control or simply Quality.) I wondered why such a department should exist. My education as an engineer had taught me that every designer designs primarily for quality. It would be unprofessional and unethical to design something that did not have the highest quality as one of its prime design parameters. So it had never occurred to me that some other department, external to the design or manufacturing departments should exist for the purpose of inspecting or monitoring or teaching "quality" to the rest of the organization. Quality was not an add-on parameter nor a discipline of study, I felt, and it was not a legitimate activity. The existence of such a function in a corporation was an indication, I believed, that there was something very wrong with the organization.

So, some years and some jobs later, when I had summoned my courage to speak up, I began telling vice presidents and directors of Quality in companies for which I worked that "The prime mandate of a Quality department should be to work towards its disbandment through redundancy." Naturally, most of my audience was shocked by my brazen statement. But a few enlightened ones understood. Yes! A Quality department should engender throughout the whole organization such passion for excellent quality in everything that there was no longer any need for such a separate function to monitor quality, or to test for it, or to control it, or to enhance it.

I never succeeded in explicitly changing any organizations, although I can hope that I caused some people to think seriously of their roles, and perhaps to advocate for change internally. But my views broadened to the point of advocating similar views, such as:

- The prime purpose of a Recreation department should be to work toward eliminating itself, through teaching people to manage their own recreation.

- The prime purpose of a customer Training department should be to make itself redundant, through teaching designers to build on-job training and performance support[3] into products.

- The prime purpose of a Medical facility should be to minimize its need for existence, through teaching people to eat nutritiously and to adopt healthy lifestyles.

And, ultimately:

- The prime purpose of a Human Resources department should be to reduce an organization's need for it, through distributing its function throughout the organization.

These extreme views that I hold should not be implemented literally, as self-annihilation, but should be used to set fundamental goals to aim for. Thus, goals should be set to eliminate, say 90% of a Human Resources department, or perhaps 85% of a Training department, and so on, over a specified timeframe, say four or five years. I would never advocate totally eliminating a department, but simply to aim towards that goal.

Now, one could ask how would the work get done if HR, quality, and customer training departments become greatly scaled down? I suggest a carefully planned transition to a new business model: one centered around the modern notion

---

3   Various resources are now available in the area of performance support. See, for example, my book *Performance Support Solutions: Achieving Business Goals Through Enabling User Performance*: Bloomington, IN: Trafford Publishing, 2002.

of performance support. This means that the performance of workers is supported at the time and place of need. When a person needs skills and knowledge to perform a job, the workplace environment coaches him through the necessary steps. When quality needs to be ensured, the development infrastructure analyzes the design and reports compliance with standard quality parameters. When personnel functions need to be considered, the corporate policy and procedure infrastructure is accessible in a context-sensitive manner for assistance.

Some good news in this respect is the modern move toward standardization of business processes. One often sees businesses proudly proclaiming their accreditation with ISO (International Organization for Standardization) 9000-series and related standards.

The key point here is for each of us to accept personal (and professional) responsibility in these areas. Each of us needs to ask fundamental questions of the institutions that we encounter. What should be their prime purposes? Should they exist? Can we improve them?

I believe that we each have the responsibility in our workplaces always to ask whether there is a better way of doing things.

Unthinking animals accept the status quo. Thinking humans should accept the responsibility to question the status quo, and to think about what is the right thing to do in each situation.

Calculators in schools

Using electronic calculators without understanding the problem at hand or calculating the approximate answer to be expected can lead to unanticipated disasters.

When hand calculators were first allowed in schools, back in the 1980s, I was annoyed. What an abominable misinterpretation of what schools were about! It showed a fundamental misunderstanding of the purpose of education, to my way of thinking.

I learned a very valuable lesson somewhere in my schooling: always estimate the answer to a problem, and then compare the calculated answer to that estimate for closeness. If the two were close, then the calculation was likely trustworthy. But if the two were greatly different, then we should be very suspicious of the calculation or the estimate, and should redo the work. That lesson has served me well for the rest of my life, both in my professional work and in my handling of household finances and other numerical work.

My objection to the practice of allowing calculators in schools is based on my view of the theory of education and training. Training is for developing skills. Education is for acquiring knowledge. Together they are for nurturing wisdom.

The school system, in my mind, should achieve a reasonable balance between training and education. This means:

- becoming *trained in performing the skills* for various topics (such as language, mathematics, and history), to the point of competently performing operations in those topics (such as fluent speaking, writing, and reading; correctly solving arithmetic and other mathematical problems; and correctly identifying historical dates, trends, and events), and at the same time,

- becoming *educated in understanding a body of knowledge* about those topics and related ones (such as the topics listed above), to the point of competently building on that knowledge to acquire more of it (such as recognizing cultural and literary patterns, understanding the theoretical foundations of mathematical thinking, and making discerning judgments based on historical knowledge).

Now, that's a tall order. I don't think that ordinary public schools can actually achieve such a balance. But they should at least strive to do so. The key point is *balance*. Don't train exclusively, even though it is easier and gives easily measured results. Don't educate exclusively, even though it is purer and develops more discerning citizens. Do both, in a balanced mode.

The title of this article refers to using calculators in schools. The chief thing that I want to discourage is having students (or anyone) use a calculator and blindly trust the answer that it provides without questioning whether it is the correct answer. Naively accepting the result opens the user to the error of ridiculous answers, perhaps due to an input error or to a machine malfunction, and thus committing an even larger error if that result is used in a subsequent operation. A bridge might collapse. (Now there's civic responsibility!) A bank account might be overdrawn. An innocent target might be struck. A medical prescription strength might be grossly over-calculated, perhaps resulting in a tragic death. A spacecraft on its way to Mars might become lost.

The important point is to strike a balance between skills and knowledge, training and education. Estimating an answer is an act of an educated person: one takes a higher-level view of the problem, appeals to some theory of its domain, and comes up with an approximate answer. Calculating the answer is an act of a trained person: one mechanically operates a system to compute the answer. Comparing the two answers is an act of a wise person: one makes an intelligent judgment to decide how to proceed.

Calculators provide only one example of a mechanical or electronic tool that can be used after being trained to use it, but which can be used much more intelligently after an appropriate education. Other examples include:

- driving a vehicle (training in its operation, education in traffic and other rules)

- using a computer application (training in its usage, education in discerning when and why to use it)

- taking pictures with a camera (training in its functions, education in picture composition, exposure, artistic effects, and so on)

- using accounting tools (training in their operation, education in choosing the right tool and in interpreting results)

- and many others.

Tools that provide a mechanical or intellectual advantage for their users are not bad *per se*. What is bad is their uneducated usage. Allow calculators or other tools in schools only with a proper balance between training and education.

I believe that it is our civic responsibility to watch for any imbalances between training and education that we may encounter in life, and to work constructively towards a proper balance. I urge you to think carefully of any such situations that you find, and then to do the right thing.

When at war, sacrifice at home

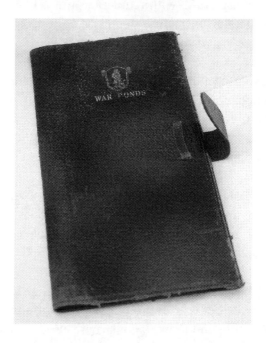

Most young people will not recognize the notion of "War Bonds" or the above war bond folder. That's because most young people have not experienced war or the notion of supporting the war effort from home. War bonds were a widely-used means of financing the military campaigns, and governments would publish advertisements urging people to buy war bonds to support the effort. I use this image to symbolize sacrificing when a country is at war.

My country, Canada, is at war. In 2009-10 Canada had more than 2000 troops deployed in Afghanistan, fighting for various humanitarian purposes, such as helping that country modernize in terms of human rights, democracy, and freedom from oppression. But do I see the citizens of Canada sacrificing their lifestyles at home in order to support our troops in a far-off country? No!

Similarly, the United States of America, is also at war. They have troops in Iraq and other countries. Do we see American citizens sacrificing at home? No!

Such a situation can be observed in various other countries: Great Britain, France, and so on.

I am too young to remember it personally, but I've certainly heard the stories and read the histories of sacrifice during the major wars of the past century. In support of the "War Effort" people at home would ration food, they would use government-organized food stamps to buy groceries, they would mend socks rather than buy new ones, they would buy war bonds, and they would patriotically sacrifice many luxuries in order to enable the country's economy to support their military in the distant conflict.

Do we see such sacrifice today? Think about it. Our me-first, immediate gratification, fun-preoccupied society is too busy seeking superficial satisfaction to care about something so grubby as fighting for freedom, whether for other people or for our own citizens.

Is this attitude a responsible one, either personal or civic? I would suggest No. As for many other aspects of our lives, we have shed our responsibility for our war efforts to someone else. We let our military personnel do the fighting, dying, and peace enforcement. We let our governments do the policy making for wars, and the funding of them through taxing us. We let someone else do the dirty work. Only a few people protest for change. And the rest of us ignore the war, or feel as if it is too distant and therefore won't affect us. At least in the war bond days, people sacrificed at home. But not in recent times.

Civic responsibility is missing here. Like an abandoned shopping cart, it is gone.

But it doesn't have to be that way. Please don't abandon this one. Think deeply about it and decide for yourself. Do you support war efforts or condemn them? Decide, and then take responsible action accordingly.

Drive responsibly

The glamour of irresponsible driving has become a religion. Movies worship it. Advertisers exalt it. Peer pressure promotes it. We have thrown caution to the wind.

Traffic these days is heavier than ever, and it can be quite easy to become frustrated while driving. Many people drive rudely, far too rapidly and dangerously, wastefully, and in a show-off, prideful manner. They transform into indecent yahoos when behind a steering wheel.

Where is the personal and civic responsibility here? Where is the sense of decency, civility, and good citizenship? Where is the perspective of one's role in the world?

Look at this situation as a zero-sum game. This means that the sum of all of a system's gains and losses is zero. Driving a car involves gains to one's personal abilities and achievements: one can go farther, carry more groceries, go to distant places more quickly, and so on. It also involves losses to resources: petroleum and other resources get depleted, the atmosphere gets polluted, one's finances and health get drained, and so forth. Is the sum zero? Do the gains balance the losses?

My belief is that the losses far outweigh the gains. The gains are few and only for a short term. However, the losses are not only the ones listed above, but also various fundamental and intangible items, including the loss of one's sense of personal responsibility to care for the world. This loss must not be underestimated, for it detracts from one's core self at the level of one's conscience. If you drive wastefully, you may also very likely become more wasteful in other aspects of your life. The habit will tend to grow. By contrast, if you drive prudently, you may also become more prudent in other aspects of your life. That habit will also tend to grow.

In our modern society, driving a car has become far more than simply achieving transportation. It has evolved into a status symbol, a means of self-affirmation, a sense of freedom and thrill, a mark of achievement, a means of picking up girls and guys, an advertisement of one's wealth, and various other symbols. But it has also become a burden on one's finances, a responsibility to maintain, a weapon of destruction, a noisemaker, a generator of polluted air, a drain on the earth's petroleum and other resources, a burden to be the chauffeur for others who do not have a car, and various other such negative consequences.

And it is expensive! Would you believe that the full cost of car ownership and driving is in the range of 30 to 40 cents per kilometre of driving? Try calculating it for yourself.

Here is an example of calculating the total cost of car ownership. Let us assume that we purchase a new car for $25,000, and that we amortize that amount over five years. For simplicity, let's ignore the cost of borrowing that money, that is, the interest on a loan. Assume further that we drive 20,000 km per year, amounting to 100,000 km over the five year period that we are considering. For gas consumption, assume that the car uses five litres of gas per 100 km (an excellent usage for a modern compact car), and that gas costs one dollar per litre (a conservative amount). Now we can calculate:

- Purchase: $25K / 100,000 km = 25 cents/km
- Gas: 5 litres / 100 km x 100,000 km x $1 / litre / 100,000 km = 5 cents/km
- Maintenance: Assume $1000 / year x 5 years / 100,000 km = 5 cents/km
- Insurance: Assume $1000 / year x 5 years / 100,000 km = 5 cents/km

Total cost of car ownership = 40 cents/km of driving, approximately.

You can perhaps do better than that, but I would bet not much better. Think about that the next time that someone offers to reimburse you for just the gas when you give him a drive or lend him your car. If that is all that he reimburses you, then you are being remarkably generous.

Really think about the responsibilities and costs of car ownership and driving, examining both the positive and negative consequences, and seriously ponder the personal responsibility and costs that driving entails. I believe that you will make the sobering choice to drive responsibly.

Also think about how you get around. Do you really need a car? How about using public transit or bicycling? Or what about a membership in a car sharing agency? Perhaps you could consider the advantages of living close to where you work and shop. Ultimately, you may think seriously about a fundamental lifestyle management to address transportation issues, such as career choice, where to live, and personal balance among home life, job, and general interests.

(See also "Why are gas prices so high? Drive the speed limit" on page 36.)

Delaying for latecomers

This article is about latecomers to training and other meetings. Whenever I think of training, I think of dog obedience training. So here is a cute illustration of a dog training its mistress to point upwards.

"Let's wait a few more minutes for those who are late!"

Have you heard those words from numerous instructors of training sessions, leaders of seminars, chairmen of meetings, teachers, professors, managers, and so on? I have, lots of times. And, I suspect, so have you.

Don't you just hate it?

Why should we penalize the earlycomers because of the poor time management of the latecomers? Shouldn't we reward the good behaviour of those who are there on time by starting on time? Shouldn't we train the latecomers to arrive on time by making them miss the first few minutes of the event?

I did that during my years as a technical trainer. I would announce to the class at the posted start time something like,

"We will start the class on time, as a reward to you who are here, ready to go. To wait for the latecomers would be an insult to you."

Recently I heard of a training department making an even grosser blunder. A class was cancelled, ten minutes into its designated time, because not enough students had shown up. This event, an information session, took place at an organization where a trainer had been hired to give orientation lectures about some new corporate procedures for part-time staff. Five employees had arrived at the classroom, but the organizers had expected twenty. Each of those part-time staff had made special arrangements to be there. They might have cancelled some other appointment in order to attend. They likely made arrangements on their home front, transported themselves to the building, perhaps paid a parking fee, and otherwise made the effort to attend. And the session was cancelled, due to poor attendance! What an enormous insult, inconvenience, and inhumane disgrace!

And, guess what was the topic of the information session? "Treating clients with respect"! Can you imagine a worse example to set for such a session than to treat the clients—the students—with such utter disrespect as to cancel the class, blatantly ignoring the effort and expense that each person had expended just to show up?

Of course, this one incident by itself is not worth taking up two pages in a chapter titled "Civic Responsibility". But the broader considerations do make it worthwhile. Consider your own civic responsibility to your clients, your family, your neighbours, your acquaintances. Think carefully about the logistics of events, especially from their point of view. Think about the planning that they had to do to participate in your event. Be aware of the impact of any agenda changes that you impose on them by surprise. Be especially considerate when planning for the demands of time that you put on them.

Please don't make abandoned shopping carts of your clients, friends, and so on. Respect the time arrangements that you had agreed upon, and thereby respect those people. Do the right thing.

Thirty-nine trillion dollars . . . and counting

Caution: Scary article. The amount of debt that the world is carrying is beyond normal comprehension. One can visualize the Earth being overwhelmed by a mountain of debt, a swarm of paper that becomes worthless, a choking of all lifeforms from our precious planet.

Would you believe that the global public debt is more than $39 trillion? Yes, believe it! As of late 2010, the sum total of the money that all the governments owed to each other and to various lending institutions was more than thirty-nine trillion US dollars[4]. And it is growing at well over two trillion dollars per year.

---

4   Reported by *The Economist* in various articles. See the remarkable website   www.economist.com/content/global_debt_clock   for   an

This is a situation that has been allowed (by us) to grow into these staggering levels. Now, I'm not an economist, and I'm not even familiar with elementary economic theory. But I do know what debt means, and I don't want any part of it.

Consider just your household finances. Debt is the amount of money you owe to other people or organizations, typically for things such as a mortgage or a bank loan for a large expenditure.

Deficit is the amount of money you spend, during a particular time period, that exceeds your income for that period. The debt increases each time period by adding the deficit to it.

Knowing your deficit and debt levels enables you to develop a household budget for the next year that addresses how you want to manage your debt. You can set a goal, for example, that you want to be totally out of debt in, say, three years. To do so, you may need to manage your household expenses so that you run a surplus (the opposite of a deficit) each year, in order to reduce your debt to zero in the specified timeframe.

Now, let us consider government, that is, public, debt. In modern times, it has become acceptable for governments to have deficit budgets. Thus, the public debt rises. Governments have a huge source of income, through taxes. And they have a huge source of money, through printing more of it. Increasing taxes causes unpopularity, which is a curse for governing parties. Printing more money causes inflation, which undermines future financial stability. But governments all over the world

---

interactive depiction of the world's countries and their public debt, their public debt per person, and other related economic measures.

keep letting their debt level increase, primarily to stay popular, and thus in power.

And now we are to the point that all the governments of the world owe to their various lenders a staggering thirty-nine trillion dollars! When will it ever end? Let's look at a few examples of public debt at the end of 2010:

Table: Global Public Debt, 2010, (Approximate numbers)
(Source, *The Economist* website, cited earlier)

	Public Debt ($ trillion)	Public Debt per Person ($ thousand)
World	39	6
Japan	10	82
USA	9	28
France	2	32
Germany	2	29
Canada	1	37

Can you believe some of those numbers? Every person in the world, all 7 billion of us, owe about six thousand dollars, if we averaged the global debt over the total world's population. The people in western, developed countries such as Canada, the USA, France, and Germany owe in the range of $25,000 to $40,000 to their own governments as their share of their country's public debt. Pity the unfortunate people in Japan, who owe more than $80,000 each for Japan's public debt. And the global public debt is increasing, not decreasing! Again, when will it ever end?

How and why did we ever let this situation get so out of hand? Did it just sneak up on us and surprise us? Or has the public debt been increasing for many years? I believe that the latter situation is the correct one.

The following excerpt from *The Economist* website mentioned earlier is enlightening:

> Does it matter? After all, world governments owe the money to their own citizens, not to the Martians. But the rising total is important for two reasons. First, when debt rises faster than economic output (as it has been doing in recent years), higher government debt implies more state interference in the economy and higher taxes in the future. Second, debt must be rolled over at regular intervals. This creates a recurring popularity test for individual governments, rather as reality TV show contestants face a public phone vote every week. Fail that vote, as the Greek government did in early 2010, and the country can be plunged into imminent crisis. So the higher the global government debt total, the greater the risk of fiscal crisis, and the bigger the economic impact such crises will have.

Who's to blame? I maintain that we are. Most of us stood back and watched, either consciously or unconsciously, as our governments continued to strike deficit budgets year after year, and now we are in a huge mess that will be very, very painful to correct. Yes, we entrust our elected representatives to manage our public affairs with wisdom. But, no, we cannot just relax and let them do irresponsible things with our economies. Each of us has a civic responsibility to speak up and get our government policies back on track.

Think about this dreadful situation. Then do the right thing.

Vote

Voting is the fundamental right of a free society. That right must be cherished.

Things are bad, aren't they?

The list of things that need fixing is huge: the economy, the environment, levels of unemployment, corruption, hospital funding, child poverty, homelessness, ….

Every one of us likely has some idea of how to address some of the items on the list: by taking political action, by anarchy, by bribery, by lobbying, by organizing support groups and pressing for change, by getting elected to a legislative body and initiating changes in laws, by forming a business and taking corporate action, and by all sorts of other means. In extreme cases, that's what one must do. However, in most cases, because we are juggling the demands of job, family life, personal interests, safety, and morality, we delegate to our political legislative members to act on our behalf.

This is where voting comes in. Your elected official represents you in forming government policy. Your civic responsibility is to choose those representatives well. This means understanding the issues, forming your own opinions, learning which candidates will best represent your views, perhaps supporting such candidates in various ways, and voting in elections.

It seems clear that a large proportion of people do not care who represents them. For example:

- In the past sixty years, voter turnout in American federal elections has averaged in the 40% to 60% range.

- In Canada during the same period, the voter turnout for federal elections ranged from a high of about 80% in the 1960s to a low of less than 60% in 2008.

- In France, the corresponding turnouts dropped from 80% to 60%.

- In the UK, it was from over 70% to less than 60%.[5]

Do the right thing: Vote for the candidate that best represents you and your policies at each level of government. Voting acknowledges and enhances our personal and civic responsibility.

5   Various sources, primarily the International Institute for Democracy and Electoral Assistance.

Smokers' entitlement has got to go!

It's hard to believe that at one time smoking was considered sophisticated. Furthermore, there seems to be a sense of entitlement that many smokers have developed to take frequent and long work breaks to have a smoke.

Smokers think that they are entitled to take frequent work breaks to feed their smoking habit.

Don't you think that practice is unfair to all the other workers, who don't have such a habit to feed?

I get annoyed whenever I see a group of people standing around in a cluster in front of some building, smoking, chatting, happy. Especially annoying for me is to see such a group in which the people should know better, or who should set a better role model, for example, when they cluster in front of a school or a hospital.

Consider the loss of work productivity for such a group. Typically, each such smoker will start thinking of taking the smoke break perhaps ten minutes in advance, thus being distracted from work. He will perhaps phone one of more of his colleagues to arrange to meet outside for their break. He will likely close down or somehow put on hold the work he is doing, put on a coat and outdoor clothes in cold weather, and walk some minutes to the outdoor meeting spot. Another few minutes might transpire, while the group waits for all its members. Then they will perhaps start the official timing of their fifteen-minute break. One or two cigarettes get consumed, and lots of cheery camaraderie gets shared. Then, the group breaks up after somewhat more than their allotted time, people drift back to work, possibly dropping by to chat with some others, and finally arrive back at their workplaces, get adjusted, reopen the work, and are finally back to work, perhaps a half-hour or more after their initial interruption. (To be fair, there are lots of smokers who try their best not to misuse their smoking break privilege. Good for them!)

Meanwhile, their non-smoking co-workers have continued to do their own jobs, while picking up the slack caused by the smokers' absences, by answering phones, taking messages, being interrupted, and perhaps feeling resentment.

An approximate cost of each smoker's break can be computed as follows. We will use a loaded labour rate of approximately $50 per hour per employee. This accounts not only for a basic salary of about $25 per hour, but also for all the overhead, benefits, and so on, which typically double a salary. ($50 is a conservative number, and could be $100 or more in some organizations.) Assume that the total lost productivity per smoker per session is 30 minutes, plus another 15 minutes impact on someone else who picks up the slack. Thus we have ¾ hour times $50 per hour, or about $37.50 per smoker per session. Suppose there are two sessions per day (a conservative assumption), thus making about $75 per smoker per day. Now, there are about 220 working days per year (allowing for vacations, sicknesses, weekends, holidays, training sessions, and so on), thus totaling $75 times 220, making about $16,500 per year. If an organization has ten smokers behaving as described here, then it loses about $165,000 per year due to all those smoking breaks.

Now, if we consider all the intangible, ancillary results of this smoking, such as health impacts due to smoking and second-hand smoke, business impact due to setting a poor role model in the community, indirectly teaching students bad examples in schools, impact on morale (and thus on business performance) among the non-addicted workers, and so on, it is easy to see that more than a million dollars per year could be wasted by an organization due to the entitlement that smokers feel.

Why don't we get those smokers to pay for such lost productivity? Why don't we penalize them with a reduced salary or a "smoker's tax"? Why don't we reward non-smokers with bonuses or a salary increase, to compensate them for their good behaviour?

Clearly, by not making such financial compensation, we as organizations and as a society are condoning and supporting such financial losses.

This situation has got to stop. Smokers have got to regain a sense of personal and civic responsibility. And the organizations have got to regain a sense of corporate responsibility.

Do the right thing. If you smoke, can you quit? Can you cut down by 50%, or perhaps 100% during work time?

Again, to be fair, I must admit that there are many smokers who simply cannot give up smoking. For them, the habit is not for pleasure, but due to a sickness. I feel sorry for them. But I also feel sorry for those who are impacted by their habit, such as their co-workers and others as described above.

I have stated my views here in a rather strong manner, but my intent is to ask us all to think seriously about our personal and civic responsibility.

It is likely a good thing that I do not have the power to implement my ideas in a unilateral manner!

The woman is always right

Agreement between a man and a woman can be achieved in many ways. This article suggests the best way, based on respect for the natural energies that drive the different decision-making processes of men and women.

I regret that I didn't understand this earlier in my life: in any sincere man-woman partnership, such as a marriage, the woman is always right.

Now that's a huge statement! It is controversial, open to misinterpretation, seemingly sexist, cosmic in its significance, accusable of triteness and of being a cop-out, and perhaps silly. Coming from a woman, the statement could be considered driven by a feminist agenda. Coming from a man, it could be considered preposterous, misled, and henpecked. But I believe it.

The reason I believe that women are always right has to do with the different ways that men and women make decisions.

Men are predisposed to use left-brain thinking, which means using logical analysis, and inductive reasoning: taking particular knowledge and expanding it to be more general. This style is useful in many circumstances, but it is nearly always based on incomplete information, since all of the information about a situation is rarely available.

Women tend to use right-brain thinking, which means using logical synthesis, and deductive reasoning: recognizing general patterns and applying them to particular situations. This is women's *intuition*. Intuition taps into the infinite wisdom of the universe and therefore has access to all knowledge. For example, intuition can see what will happen in the future, whereas logical analysis might never predict some specific, relevant future event.

In short, men tend to use their heads and women tend to use their hearts. Information available to the head is limited, often leading to ill-informed decisions. Information available to the heart is unlimited, and so decisions based on using the heart are mostly right.

My point here is not to suggest that women are better than men, or vice versa. They are simply different. They were designed to be different, and the manufacturing process is generally true to the design. The differences should be celebrated and honoured.

So, in an ideal joint decision-making situation, both partners bring their natural strengths to the conversation.

- The woman listens attentively to the man's logical arguments and recognizes the integrity with which he presents them. The man listens attentively to the woman's intuitive opinions and recognizes their integrity.

• Each encourages the other to develop and hone their natural skills, knowledge, and capabilities, and they teach each other enough of their own innate methods to gain mutual appreciation.

• Finally, they should reach a consensus on the decision. The woman is confident (and the man should encourage her to be confident) to speak from her heart boldly. The man is humble enough (and the woman should encourage him to be humble) to recognize that the woman is always right.

Of course many grey areas exist in real situations. Some men are more intuitive and some women are more rational. Also, I have written from an idealized point of view, for example: "sincere ... partnership" and "intuition ... has access to all knowledge". In real situations, there might be some lack of sincerity, pride might interfere, intuition might be wrongly interpreted, and other such tendencies might mess up my nice, clean theory. But I am convinced that if each partner in a relationship can do their very best to take the high road with integrity and sincerity, then each of them will agree that the woman is always right.

And, of course, we should recognize that "always" is impossible, so a more realistic title could perhaps be "The woman is nearly always right!" but I like the snappiness of my chosen title. And, I'll bet that (nearly) all women would agree with me.

I include this article in this chapter on civic responsibility because it belongs here. Recognizing that the woman is always right is one of our civic responsibilities, and it has the potential to save our society. Happy relationships and families make for stable civilizations.

Do the right thing! If you are a man, defer to your female partner; you can learn a lot. If you are a woman, hold your ground; you are very likely right.

(If a woman had written this article, it would not have its deficiencies; it would be correct.)

Interlude: A conversation - 1

"Do you know Bezanson?"

"Which one? Do you mean the author?"

"The very one!"

"Yes, I have been following his evolution. His development seems to be on track. He is a bit idealistic and often has his head in the clouds, but his intentions are noble. Why do you ask about him?"

"Do you think that he will succeed?"

The two men talked—No, not men, but formerly men. They were entities on the spirit plane. Past masters. Advanced adepts, now having responsibility for helping mankind survive and evolve.

They looked out on the cosmos, to Earth, down to humanity.

"Succeed? What is success? Will he win a lottery? Will he get the girl? Will he save humanity?"

"Come on! You know what I mean!"

"OK! Well … No! I don't think he has the slightest chance to turn around mankind's inexorable descent into depravity and self-annihilation!"

What a gloomy thought, mused Zenoch. *How can he be so negative?*

Netherfeld was convinced of his prognosis. Humans were a lost cause and beyond helping. Why bother trying to save them?

The two ascended masters came from different traditions. They had evolved on Earth to very advanced spiritual stages, to *self-mastery.* They were now part of that great Fraternity of Light that oversaw humanity's continued development. Zenoch was an optimist. Netherfeld was a pragmatist.

Zenoch had expected such a response from his partner. He continued, "But we must hold out hope for them. After all, we were humans at one time, and we will likely be so again."

"You speak the truth, my old friend. In my cheerier moments, I would agree with you. But why waste hope on a lost cause?" Netherfeld had been hopeful at one time, but he had gradually become more and more realistic about humanity's future.

They spoke to each other not in the English language, and not even with words, but by thought forms, by intuitive impressions, by spiritual communication. Over their time on the spiritual plane on which they now dwelt, they had a great many conversations about their mutual charge. They were part of the Earth Contingent. Others looked after other planets, the incomprehensibly vast number of other planets, with their various and diverse life forms.

"But hope is what we must have," pleaded Zenoch.

"Yes, I know all that," Netherfeld responded. "But sometimes one must accept reality by analyzing the facts, and put one's efforts where they can achieve worthwhile results."

"So would you simply give up on all of them?"

Netherfeld thought for a while. He wasn't really advocating giving up on human beings. He was simply arguing in favour of putting energy into helping civilizations on other planets that were more likely to evolve and thrive with some hope of success.

"No," he responded, reluctantly and with a sigh of resignation. "I would just like to leave them alone for a while to see if they can survive without our help."

The two of them mused silently for some time. The term "for a while" was beyond their experience. And "for some time" was also foreign to them. Time had no meaning for them, but it seemed as if some time had passed. Indeed, they had risen to a level where they understood the truth that all advanced mystics knew: Time did not exist. But when they talked about their charges, earth's human beings, they had to speak in such terms as evolution, growth, development, and so on, all of which implied some sort of passage of time. They knew, of course, that it was all an illusion. And, having been human beings a great many times, they were able to understand the illusion, and to talk about it without actually experiencing it.

They could observe earth and all its living forms there. They didn't use eyes, of course, because they did not occupy bodies that had eyes. They were in a spirit form, and they retained some of the personal characteristics that they had in their last few incarnations on earth. They were best described as *soul personalities*, in the sense that they were part of the Universal Soul, but they had distinct and separate personalities. Their observing and seeing was done by psychic means, intuitively, mentally.

Also, they did not look "down" on the earth, but more like "out" at it. The notion of "down" had no meaning for them. Their spiritual plane permeated all of the universe, and they could see everywhere at once.

Netherfeld picked up the discussion. "Just look at the many ways that mankind has mismanaged his beautiful island home that is at the same time a perfect, resilient habitation, but is also very fragile. First he overpopulates it. Then he pollutes it. Next he depletes it of its non-renewable resources. Finally, he allows its atmosphere to retain heat, causing the polar ice to melt. And those are just the big things."

"Yes," continued Zenoch, "I agree that mankind has been a poor steward for his island home. He has also been a disaster to his fellow-humans. Killings, pillaging, robberies, vandalizing, terrorism, and on and on. I can see how you would lose hope in ever seeing mankind turn around and mend his awful ways."

"And this Bezanson! He actually thinks that he can make a difference. Ha! How can one lonely man tame a wild monster?"

As they talked and watched for nearly a full earth day, at least another twenty thousand children died of starvation, five thousand people died as a result of various wars and conflicts, two thousand people died of complications resulting from smoking tobacco, and fifty species of animals and plants went extinct.[6]

Zenoch continued, "But Bezanson is not working alone. Many of his fellow humans agree with him. And, after all, he has our help. And we serve the Light!"

"Ah, well! Thanks for the reminder. You are right. But it gets harder and harder to become motivated to our mission."

"Yes, of course it's hard. But that's why two of the very best were chosen for the job. You and I must not falter under our burden and our responsibility. Always and constantly, we must continue to send inspirations and good guidance to Bezanson and the many others who feel motivated to serve the Light also."

Netherfeld mumbled to himself, and muttered, and stewed. But his partner was right, he had to admit. No matter how bad it got, they must not ever give up.

"OK. You're right! Let me get back on track.

"Where did they go wrong?" he asked. "How did they ever let the situation get so bad? How did we ever lose our influence and let them travel so very far down a destructive path?"

Zenoch paused, to let his friend mutter for a bit, and, he hoped, to come back to his senses. Even soul personalities,

---

6   Approximations based on statistics reported in Matthew White, "Source List and Detailed Death Tolls for the Primary Megadeaths of the Twentieth Century", necrometrics.com/20c5m.htm and various other online sources

pure and ethereal though they might be, can be prone to some forgetfulness, gloominess, and despondency.

Indeed, Zenoch and Netherfeld were discovering that a hierarchy of support existed not only from the spirit plane to the physical, but also on the spirit plane itself. Just as they supported and encouraged their human charges, there were higher-level soul personalities supporting and encouraging them. And still higher-level ones providing support for more junior ones, and so on. The image occurred to them, from their times on Earth, of a hierarchy of Angels, Archangels, Virtues, Cherubim, Seraphim, and others.

Gently and tenderly, he spoke, "We've talked of these things before, haven't we, Netherfeld, my dear friend?"

"Yes! And I had forgotten for a moment. I'm sorry."

"That's OK. You're allowed to slip a bit. After all, I've had my faults, and you were always here to help me get back again."

"Yes, my friend. I guess that's why we were paired up to work as partners. It was a good decision, and it is a good structure."

They paused, to collect their thoughts and memories.

Zenoch summarized their conclusions that they had reached from previous discussions. "So, the chief reason that mankind has neglected proper stewardship for their world is that they have lost their sense of value for higher principles, for a higher purpose in life, for something greater than themselves. They have 'fallen', and their literature is filled with stories and myths of their Fall, but they have not risen again. And the reason that they have not risen is that they have lost their sense of the Divine—their vision of God."

"Good summary," agreed Netherfeld. "Further, the great majority of those human beings are still stuck in their centuries-old myths about God as a supernatural being in their own image, omniscient and omnipotent, dispensing judgments all the time. And they developed sects and cults and branches of religion with different views of the same God, and fought wars in his name. No wonder they are spiraling downwards away from the Divine, towards annihilation!"

"Yes, no wonder at all. But, speaking of wonder, that's also what they have lost ... a sense of wonder."

"Bang on! You're right! In fact, that is what I think of when you mention a sense of the Divine—it's a sense of wonder for the preciousness of life, for the amazing workings of the universe, and for the enormity of creation and its evolution."

"So, what are we going to do about it all?" asked Zenoch, partly with exasperation, but also partly with great hope. He and his partner, indeed, all of the ascended masters worked from the spirit plane for the betterment and evolution of Life, and the growth and development of all the life forms in the universe: serving the Light. All of these soul personalities had spent most of their time in meditation, sending constructive, healing, inspirational thoughts and impressions to their charges on their various planets, constantly leading them towards Good and away from Evil, constantly urging them to use their free wills to make positive choices, to reach higher, to strive for the best, to arise once again from their various falls, and to regain their sense of the Divine.

They knew, of course, that the Divine—God—was not a personal being open to persuasion for performing miracles. God is the impersonal wisdom and energy that dispassionately and with complete indifference to individual life forms creates, sustains, and manifests the various laws of Nature.

"God equals Nature!" proclaimed Zenoch. "As you and I know, and as all advanced mystics know, God is not a personal, masculine being who can be convinced to change its mind and make miracles happen simply because someone prays to it. God is neutral, as well as both masculine and feminine, and it is equivalent to the sum total of all the Laws of Nature, both physical laws and spiritual laws.

"So that gives me an idea of what we must do about this dreadful situation!" he continued, with evident excitement. "We must help all the people whom we can influence to grow up and to start thinking for themselves, as mature humans. We must lead them away from their priesthoods and the obsolete, confinements of their stifling religions, and towards an open-minded realization that God is not personal, but impersonal; not capricious, but constant; not supernatural, but Nature itself!"

"Very inspiring," noted Netherfeld, "but isn't that what we've been doing all along?"

"Yes, you are right, of course. But we need a new approach." Zenoch was trying to be upbeat and optimistic, hoping that he would think of a fresh idea, a teacher striving to keep just one step ahead of his student.

"OK, how about this," suggested Netherfeld. "We could do a mass blitz to all humanity, by recruiting all the other ascended masters to join us for a focused campaign, say, to convince people of God's impersonality."

Zenoch considered this idea. He acknowledged that it was good, but not great. "You're on the right track, my friend. But let's think of the situation from the perspective of the people we want to reach. We need to catch their attention somehow— something that impacts their lifestyles ...."

"I know! How about convincing them that they'll only have one car per family, rather than two or more, if they don't clean up their act? Or no more television? Or something shocking like that?"

"Bingo! You're onto it!" exclaimed Netherfeld. "Lifestyle ... Yes! Even *Life itself*! Yes—that's it—They will not even have life, when it is time for them to reincarnate, if they allow the earth to die!

"So *reincarnation* is the key! We should work on convincing them that reincarnation is a spiritual truth, and that the law of Karma governs how it operates!"

Zenoch was delighted. "Excellent! That's perfect!"

"But, as we have discussed many times before," Netherfeld reminded Zenoch, "People don't want to know the Truth. They would rather hide behind the comforting structures of religion or other supernatural beliefs. They would rather not face the truth about reincarnation. They prefer to shirk the tough job of accepting personal responsibility for seeking to understand the spiritual truths of the universe. They would rather let priests and others tell them what to believe and how to conduct their lives."

"So you're saying that we'll have a tough job convincing them about reincarnation."

"Yes. It will be difficult."

"But, fortunately, we don't need to convince all seven billion of them, but just those who have grown tired of conventional religious teachings so that they are hungry to know the Truth. They want to think for themselves, seeking to understand the big picture. Once they become convinced, they will tell others and spread the word. Their voice will be added to those of the Buddhists and others who already know that reincarnation is an actual fact."

"Yes! You're right. And I think that this is the only chance we will get to save humankind and their earth."

The two soul personalities paused and basked for a while in the good feelings of having developed a plan for saving their precious charges.

"So let's begin immediately!" Zenoch knew that another day must not pass, with another twenty thousand children dying of starvation. "We must focus our energies on sending to all people images of their earlier experiences of former incarnations. They will receive intuitive insights into a larger view of themselves. They will have dreams, sudden flashes of deep memory, and unexpected impulses that awaken their curiosity about their lives."

"Yes," continued Netherfeld, "And when they realize the truth about their former incarnations and of more to come, they will gradually realize that the real reason that they should be responsible stewards of their planet and their lives is not just to protect the environment for their children and grandchildren, but also for themselves. They will want the earth to be in good shape when they return to it, and they will want civilization to be much more civil than it is currently."

"So, my friend, we have our work cut out for us, and I believe that we have a hope of success."

"And so also does Bezanson, whom you mentioned earlier. We must help him succeed, and others like him."

Chapter 4: Using your life responsibly

This picture illustrates what might be termed "Responsible abandonment". If you must abandon your shopping carts, then move them up onto a boulevard, out of the way of traffic, causing less inconvenience for others. Such abandoners are perhaps gradually recovering, one step at a time: boulevard today, tomorrow the corral! Maybe "Creeping responsibility" could be a good title.

This chapter addresses the biggest act of irresponsibility of all: wasting your own life!

There are many ways that we can waste that most precious gift of all that we have been given: our lives. We can fail to appreciate and use our natural talents and interests, we can set poor examples for our children and others, we can occupy our time with trivialities, we can aim lower than for excellence in our endeavours, and in many other ways.

Eat the icing last

Ah, icing! I live for the icing! But what a dilemma! Eat it first or last, or a bit with each bite? Oh, the problems of modern life!

When I was young, I ate the cake first and the icing second. I still do it that way. I don't remember why I developed such a habit. I just did. I don't remember Mom or Dad teaching me to save the good part for the last. I don't remember reading about that method anywhere. It just came to me naturally.

I do remember being puzzled with people who would eat the icing first, in order to get their enjoyment first. Later I learned in high school about modern Epicureans: "Eat, drink, and be merry, for tomorrow we may die!" What a misguided attitude, I thought.

As I grew older I found more and more ways to "eat the icing last". For example, I would often reward myself with a pleasurable task after doing the unpleasant chores first.

Life is full of necessary duties, unpleasant tasks, and other forms of drudgery: buy the groceries, clean the bathrooms, teach the children, repair those breakages, pay the bills, get up early, drive to work, attend those meetings, write those reports, do the chores, visit the dentist, consult the job jar, and so on. For every one of those unpleasant items, one can easily think of some fun thing to do in its place: buy a magazine, have a nap, watch some television, quaff a beer, read a book, surf the Web, shoot some pool, play a videogame, bask in the sun, skip that meeting, … another list that goes on and on. And our modern permissive society encourages us to place more value in the pleasant list than in the unpleasant one: take a break, you deserve it, spend your money, go into debt, take that vacation, consume those goods, buy that dress, buy that car, buy that home entertainment system, …. School is abbreviated and easier. Work hours are shorter. Get trained, rather than educated. Don't bother reaching for the top. Get a job, not a career …. On and on.

Where is the discipline of life? It comes from delaying gratification, as M. Scott Peck advocated in *The Road Less Travelled*. Do the tough things first, and reward yourself with the pleasant things second. You will have earned them, that way, and they will seem so much more delicious and pleasurable!

And eventually, the unpleasant tasks will not even be unpleasant any more. That's because you will have developed the discipline to accept them, and to have power over them. The power comes from rising above them; their unpleasantness simply does not matter to you any longer.

This practice of delaying gratification is not just for the short term of rewarding yourself with some icing after eating the cake. It is actually a spiritual practice that helps you grow and evolve as a person.

The real secret is finding enjoyment in everything: making gratification not last or first, but continuous, through a contented balance in life. Such a model would suggest that each bite of cake might consist of a mixture of cake and icing.

Finding such enjoyment in life is actually a spiritual practice. For example, St. Paul, in his letter to the *Philippians*, chapter 4, verse 11 states, "I have learned, in whatever state I am, to be content." (Revised Standard Version of the Bible). Further, Buddhism teaches that "Life is suffering" as the first of the Four Noble Truths, but that suffering can be overcome by following the Eightfold Path, including Right Mindfulness and other principles of moral conduct. And the original Epicurus, contrary to how his philosophy evolved, taught the virtue of a simple life.

Spiritual responsibility will be explored in the final chapter of this book.

Cruising for the best parking spot

If only one could have a bird's-eye view of a parking lot, to help decide where to turn to find a good parking spot!

How many times have I cruised around in shopping centre parking lots, up and down the rows, searching for the optimum spot? I'd rather not tell.

The good news is that some years ago I discovered a new method of finding the optimum parking spot: taking the first spot that I saw, even if it is near the back of the parking lot. By doing so, I found that I was able to avoid the frustration, tension, and time wastage of cruising, searching, and competing for the best spot, closest to the door of the store where I was planning to shop. The extra few steps provide a bit of exercise, some fresh air, and mostly a sense of lightness, or a lack of burden, due to having made a quick decision and not worrying about getting the spot closest to the door.

And if that first parking spot that I saw happened to be close to a shopping cart corral, then so much the better. When you think of it, on departing from the store, one wants the car to be very close not to the building exit, but to the shopping cart corral for quick return of one's shopping cart.

I've been an amateur student of human behaviour for many years. A fascinating study for me has been watching drivers cruising for parking spots at shopping centres or large wholesale stores or office buildings. People will drive around and around, wasting time and gas (as I used to do), hoping to get as close as possible to the store entrance. Drivers might even hover, waiting, as I unload my groceries. Occasionally, I've seen extreme examples of such behaviour. For example, a driver would see me leaving the store with a full shopping cart, and he would follow me to my car, and sit there idling while I opened my car's trunk, unloaded my groceries, closed the trunk, wheeled the cart to the corral, returned to my car, started it up, and backed out of the parking spot. Then the driver would pull furtively into my spot. (I sometimes even imagined that he was a bit angry with me for taking so long, because I have seldom been thanked for freeing up a spot.) For all of that time, the driver ignored lots of available parking spots a few rows away.

I certainly hope that I have not behaved that way! Or if I did, then not any longer. With my newly discovered scheme of always picking the first spot that I see, especially if it is in the general vicinity of a shopping cart corral, which is where I will want to be when I have finished shopping, with that scheme, I can actually enjoy the experience. I feel somehow detached from the masses of other shoppers. I am marching to my own drummer, avoiding potential frustration and disappointments, and feeling good about myself.

I wonder if other drivers are watching my behaviour as I arrive at a parking lot, thinking perhaps that they might try that technique when they come here next time. I suspect not, but I truly hope so!

Incidentally, it is interesting to note that there are other ways to find the best parking spot. For example, I know two people who can create parking spots mentally. One visualizes the parking spot that he wants, and then it materializes, often by having a person drive away just in time from that spot. The other asks her "parking spirit" to provide her with a parking spot exactly where she wants it. That method works for her!

But for most of us, we don't have access to a parking spirit nor can we visualize strongly enough, so my advice is to take the first parking spot that you see.

Or maybe we could work on our powers of visualization, or on our imaginations.

Do the right thing for using your life responsibly. Are you spending precious time, energy, and emotions in searching for trivial things such as parking spots? If so, think about how you can free up your life by taking the first parking spot you see, and by cultivating other such forms of simplifying your life.

Making purchase decisions based solely on price

Everyone loves a sale. But selling price is only the tip of the iceberg in the overall cost of a product or service.

Sale prices are so very tempting when making a decision to purchase something. Low prices: how very seductive they are! Priced to sell: yes, exactly, priced to sell! Act now! And regret later.

I have to admit, I've been sucked in by low prices. The marketing pitch can be enormously powerful.

And yet, I've often come to regret buying only because the selling price is low!

I should know better. I've long advocated thinking about the bigger picture, and I've often argued that after-sales support is more important than initial price and the pre-sales pitch.

The key thing is to consider life-cycle costs[7]. For example, here are some of the things to consider in the life

---

7   The life-cycle of a product is its expected age before needing replacement. A personal computer might have a life-cycle of three years; a car, ten years; a pair of shoes, five years. The anticipated length of a life-cycle allows one to plan and to budget for product upgrading or replacement.

cycle of a personal computer system. But these ideas apply to buying many other products also:

- The selling price. The selling price should be low enough to be affordable and justifiable, but don't forget the cost of a maintenance contract or extended warranty, spare parts, optional accessories such as a printer or expanded memory, associated sub-products such as required software or upgraded software to be compatible with this new product, and, of course, taxes.

- The shipping price. What is the cost of shipping, transporting, receiving, and storing the product until installation, including customs, duties, and tariffs?

- The installation cost. What is the cost of unpacking the product, preparing the environment to accommodate it, studying the installation instructions, doing the installation, testing the product, and exchanging it if parts are missing or broken? Note that such cost mostly consists of your own labour and time, but these do have a dollar value, such as time taken from other projects, or driving or shipping for replacement parts.

- The commissioning cost: What is the cost of upgrading from an older product, bringing data over from the older product, retiring the older product, configuring and testing the new product, registering it for warranty, upgrading and testing related products for version compatibility, and other related costs? Again, even if you only have to account for your own time and labour, it is important to assign a value for them.

- The learning cost: What is the cost of learning to install, commission, operate, and maintain the product, along with the cost of ongoing learning for skills enhancement, performance improvement, and feature upgrades? Such costs may include formal training fees in addition to your own time.

- The operating cost: What is the cost of running and operating the product, including electrical and environmental power, supplies such as paper, spare parts, and consumables, as well as fixed and variable costs, and the support infrastructure?

- The maintenance cost: What is the cost of maintaining the product, including regular routine maintenance, troubleshooting, virus protection, diagnosing, reporting, and resolving problems, implementing fixes, system upgrades and expansion, and the opportunity cost of operating without the product while it is being repaired or replaced?

- The decommissioning cost: What will be the cost of retiring the product some years later, preparing to replace it with another one, disposing of it—especially responsible disposing through recycling—and other related costs?

All of the above points, and perhaps others as well, should be considered when making a purchase decision. Now, I admit that buying a simple product such as a pen or pencil can be analyzed along the above lines rather quickly and easily. But a new digital camera, or a new laptop computer, or a new car, or a new house, very likely deserve a thorough analysis, as above. And buying something for your own personal usage might be easily decided, but buying a set of things for use by several people, such as your family or your employees in a company, can greatly benefit from a careful analysis.

I maintain that doing a life-cycle cost analysis will very often convince you, for example, that a Macintosh computer system has a much smaller life-cycle cost than a corresponding PC has, a high-quality product from a reputable manufacturer has a much smaller life-cycle cost than a cheap product from a questionable manufacturer, and buying something from a large, stable department store will involve smaller life-cycle costs than buying from a small specialized store. Also, buying from your local country is less expensive in the long run than buying from a foreign country.

The initial selling price is just the start of the spending. Don't be fooled by it. Pay now or pay later: buy quality. Do the right thing: analyze and look well beyond the selling price of something in order to make responsible purchasing decisions.

Be thrifty

Being thrifty is a responsible way to manage your finances and live your life.

Whatever happened to thrift?

It seems to be old fashioned and uncool to be thrifty these days. Watching the way people spend money and go deeply into debt might suggest to you that they are from a different planet. How can the world continue to sustain this unthrifty human species if living beyond our means continues to be the norm?

In a recent issue of the *Templeton Report*[8] an excellent article "Whatever happened to thrift?" was included. It observed that Americans save and invest only when the economy is shrinking, but that they do the opposite when the economy is expanding: they borrow and splurge. Typically, they are not thrifty, except when forced to be so. The article cited Sir John Templeton as having advocated that thrift should

---

8   "News from the John Templeton Foundation", November 25, 2008
      —   www.templeton.org/newsroom/newsletters_and_publications/,
     navigate to "Templeton Report")

be "something like honesty, part of who you are and the way you want to be."

The Templeton Foundation has funded some study initiatives on thrift in recent years. Several impressive reports and books resulted, leading one reviewer to conclude "Thrift is not just a medicine for when we are sick. It's a practical strategy for the good life."

A *New York Times* column praised one of the initiatives (the report *For a New Thrift: Confronting the Debt Culture*) with the words "Over the past 30 years ... the social norms and institutions that encouraged frugality and spending what you earn have been undermined. The institutions that encourage debt and living for the moment have been strengthened. The country's moral guardians are forever looking for decadence out of Hollywood and reality TV. But the most rampant decadence today is financial decadence, the trampling of decent norms about how to use and harness money."[9]

This work by the Templeton Foundation lines up quite nicely with my own innate attitude about thrift. Save before buying. Use payment cards as charging rather than credit vehicles. Use accrual accounting, not cost accounting, for your household finances, as will be explained later. Fix before replacing. Save for the future. Maintain a buffer of cash to cushion the impact of hard times.

Note that being thrifty does not necessarily mean being cheap. Buying high quality or expensive items may be the right choice in the long run, as explained earlier. Similarly, being thrifty does not necessarily refer only to money. It is important

---

9   The full article is available at www.nytimes.com/2008/06/10/opinion/
      10brooks.html?_r=1&scp=1&sq=%22david%20brooks%22%20
      thrift&st=cse

to be thrifty with many aspects of life, such as your driving habits to consume gas prudently, and honing your good habits with respect to your thinking and your time.

God's gift to you is your life. Your gift to God is how you use that life.

Modern society seductively lures us away from being thrifty. But we can rise above that trap, by using our human intelligence to think rationally. When we take responsibility for our lives, managing our resources prudently, surely we must conclude that part of any decent life is the basic notion of thrift.

Use accrual accounting for your personal and home finances

Accrual accounting means saving funds to pay for your credit purchases. It is the only responsible way to account for your finances.

It always baffles me when people are surprised by the large amount that they owe on their monthly charge card statements. Their surprise is due to the fact that they don't have the funds saved to pay off the balance in full.

They follow the accounting method called Cost Accounting. When the statement arrives, they scurry around looking for funds to pay it. If there is a shortfall, they must carry over a balance until next month, attracting interest charges (quite large ones in many cases).

A smarter way to account for your finances is to use Accrual Accounting. With this method you save up for each expense that you make, such that when the statement arrives, you already have the funds saved and can pay off the balance in full.

I discovered that latter method many years ago. (Of course, I didn't invent it, but merely stumbled upon it.) My practice evolved into the following method. When we charge an amount to one of our charge card accounts, I immediately move that amount from column A (my "Main Account") to column B (my "Charge Account") in my accounting book. Column B gradually gets larger (and A smaller) with each such transaction. At any time, the value of column B matches the total value of all my outstanding charge card expenses. Eventually, when the statements come in, I can pay off the full amount of each such charge card invoice, thereby incurring no interest charges.

A further rational way of managing finances is to save a bit each month for those annual recurring expenses, such as property taxes, income taxes, and insurance premiums. In our case, I make an estimate of the annual total of such recurring expenses, and I try to move an appropriate amount each month from column A to column C (my "Tax fund"). When one of those recurring expenses becomes due, such as an insurance premium, I pay for it from column C. Reviewing the recurring expense total each year keeps it on track.

That accrual accounting method makes a great deal of sense to me. It involves using payment cards not as Credit Cards but as Charge Cards. Not only does it attract no interest charges, but it also defers payments by up to two months, allowing me to gain a small amount of interest by investing the funds. The payment card companies don't like the accounting methods of people such as myself, and I don't like their advertising the pleasures of using "credit cards".

Actually, I first heard the term "charge card" many years ago when one of the payment card companies proudly declared that they did not offer credit cards but charge cards;

they required that each customer pay in full each month the statement amount. Eventually, that company followed the example of their rivals and switched to offering credit cards. They likely found such a practice to be more lucrative.

To my way of thinking, using accrual accounting and charge cards is an efficient and practical way of living. It requires discipline and restraint, but so also do most forms of survival in the jungle of modern life, and doing so makes life more worth living, in the sense that your resources are being used in a more responsible manner.

Think carefully about how you manage your personal and household finances. The responsible thing to do is to use accrual accounting and to use those payment cards for deferring charges, not for accumulating credit.

Use your brain for a change

Rodin's The Thinker *has for more than a century represented sober pondering, meditation, concentration, and deep thinking.*

I adapted the title of this article from the book, *Using Your Brain for a Change*, which I read in the mid 1980s. It was a book about Neuro-Linguistic Programming. I love the double meaning of the title: both as a novel usage, something new, a "change", and also as a means of changing yourself, fundamental transformation of your habits, your lifestyle, your inner self view.

For this article, I use the title with both interpretations of "change".

How very often we don't use our brains! We let popular culture dictate to us what movies to see, what music to listen to, what books to read, and what TV shows to watch. We let the fashion industry tell us what clothes to wear, how to style our hair, and how to decorate our homes. We let advertisers influence us for what cars to buy, what tourist places to visit, and what food to eat. We let organized religions specify to us what to believe, how to behave, and what deities to worship. We let the mob mentality of crowds lead us into unruly behaviour, too rapid driving, and lowered moral standards. We let the media persuade us to watch rather than read, to follow rather than lead, to consume rather than save, and to comply rather than think.

For a change, why don't we use our brains?

Why do we absolve our own personal responsibility to someone else (popular culture, the fashion industry, advertisers, organized religions, crowds, media, and others) rather than using our brains for a change?

We tend to drift along, following external stimuli, rather than deliberately deciding how we want to live our lives. We can use our brains for making that change.

An example of not using our brains that has always annoyed me is the over-reliance on experience rather than reasoning. People often give advice based only on their experience, they often make decisions based on their own or others' experiences, and they often say, "Let's try it and see what happens." Behaving this way ignores our powers of reasoning. Human beings have evolved to the point that they can analyze a situation and make decisions based on theoretical conclusions, rather than depending on the "error and trial" methods of experience.

The animals learn by experience. Humans can build on that method and also learn by thinking.

To be fair, we don't all behave like sheep, following the crowd or neglecting to use our brains. You, dear reader, I hope, don't need to hear the advice in this article. If not, I am very pleased for you. Now, go forth and teach the others!

Personal responsibility: that's what I'm addressing here. Think about it. Do we want to continue the way we have been going along, or do we want to use our brains for a change?

Do it because it's right, not because a cop might be watching

A judge's gavel and books of law. Is that what motivates our behaviour?

Have you ever seen anybody look both ways to see if a police car is nearby, and then make an illegal turn? Or how about driving well beyond the speed limit at the same time as watching carefully for a police cruiser? Or sneaking an illegal jab if the referee is not watching?

Even closer to home, have you ever been guilty of doing one of those offences yourself? I know that I have done some of them, and other similar acts.

"Go ahead, I don't see a cop!" "Don't worry, the Dean is looking the other way!" "Now's a good time, nobody can see you!"

What friend would give such advice? Too many, I'm afraid.

Wrong! Wrong! Wrong!

The correct reason for doing the right thing, for driving within the speed limit, for parking only in designated spots, and for conducting your affairs legally, is not because you might get caught doing the wrong thing, but because it's right. Not because a cop might be watching, but because it's right. Not because it's the law, but because it's right.

Your conscience should be your guide, not an external sign or law or authority.

People must learn to serve their inner selves, their higher sense of ethics, their moral code, and not to serve expediency, urgency, or crowd behaviour.

Do it because it's right, not because some authority figure is watching!

Live to the east of where you work

The dawning or setting sun can be startlingly beautiful to gaze at over the water, but also viciously dangerous while driving a car when it causes your eye pupils to close down.

Don't you hate driving into the blazing sun?

In one of my early jobs I had to drive across the city squinting into the sunrise every morning and into the sunset every evening. I lived to the West of where I worked. And I resolved that in the future I would always live to the East of where I worked. That way, the sun would always be at my back during my normal commuting times.

Of course, if you work the nightshift, or travel to work in a North-South direction, you will need to make the appropriate adjustments to this guideline.

The key point here is not simply about planning your route, but to plan forward for every life decision, to consider all the variables that you can think of. Your driving direction, with respect to the morning and evening sun position, can be very important, and I use it here to illustrate one's broader responsibility in life.

Once or twice per month facing into the bright sun can be tolerated. But day after day, every working day, for years, can really get you down. And it can be dangerous, too. That leads to an even more profound point about this guidance. Driving with the sun at your back is not only about being comfortable without bright sunshine in your eyes. It is also about being calmer and more alert as you drive. And it is about being thoughtful and mindful of your situation with respect to your world: flowing with the tide rather than against it. And it is about arriving safely at your destination, for the sake of your children and your spouse and your employer and your colleagues and your friends ... and yourself. It is about being a better and more responsible person. Further, if you meditate on a still bigger picture, positioning yourself optimally with respect to the earth, the sun, your workplace, and your home attunes you to your place in the cosmos and your acknowledgment and respect for it.

So in the grand scheme of things, living to the East of where you work is an acknowledgment of your role in creation, and a decision to be an active part of the cosmos and to help to further its evolution.

Of course, another way of avoiding the sun on your regular commute is not to drive to work at all. Take the bus. Choose to live near where you work so you can walk or bicycle there. Design the circumstances of your life, as much as you are able to do so, to achieve an agreeable balance among the many parameters that you can affect.

The decision of where to live and where to work is not to be taken lightly.

As for the other articles in this book, think carefully, and then do the right thing.

How to decide

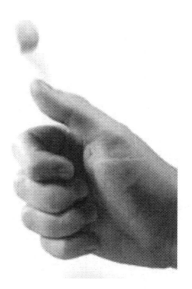

Tossing a coin is the classic way of making a decision when two options are under consideration, and you want to leave the choice to random chance. However, that's like abandoning shopping carts: abdicating your own responsibility to make decisions.

What is the best method for making decisions? I have a method that I have used with some success, and which I recommend that you try.

Now, the decisions I'm talking about here are the big ones, not the trivial ones. Deciding what to have for dessert is not a show stopper. Deciding what movie to watch is not worth agonizing over.

But whom to marry? What job to accept? Which course of study to pursue? Which religious institution to join? How to find a precious lost object? Which career path to take? Which house to buy? Which service club to join? These and other big ones are the life-altering, profound, very important decisions.

So how do we make such decisions? There are two main methods: the rational method and the irrational method.

The rational method is the modern, accepted one. It uses our intellect to analyze the situation, research various options and the underlying theory, discuss with others, use our left-brain analytical powers, perhaps even do a risk analysis, and eventually make a decision. This method was popularized with the Age of Enlightenment in the eighteenth century, and it is the method used by scientists, technological people, and most academics. It uses bottom-up[10] inductive reasoning. And it works.

The irrational method is the ancient, mystical one. It uses our intuition to synthesize solutions, find inspiration using our minds, listen for hunches, clues, and feelings, use our right-brain intuitive powers, pay attention to our dreams, perhaps seek inspiration through prayer or psychic tools and divination aids, and eventually lead to a decision. This method is very ancient, and is the method used by the artistic, feeling, visionary folk. It uses top-down deductive reasoning. And it works.

Both methods work, but for different reasons. The rational method works because it uses our conscious capabilities. The irrational method works because it uses our unconscious

---

10 Inductive reasoning means inferring some hypothesis from the particular to the general, that is, observing phenomena and formulating a model that explains them; it can be viewed as proceeding from a lower level to a higher one, hence "bottom-up". By contrast, deductive reasoning means deducing some result from the general to the particular, such as making an ethical decision based on revealed knowledge of a religious faith; it proceeds from the higher to the lower, hence "top-down".

capabilities. Both methods also fail to work sometimes, or they may not work optimally.

Specifically, the rational method by itself cannot possibly assemble all of the facts and analyze all of them, simply because some facts are unknown or unknowable. And the irrational method by itself may ignore certain important external facts or rules to develop solutions. On the other hand, the irrational method does tap into the source of all knowledge, the supreme intelligence of the universe, and thus it can build on the analysis of the rational method to lead to quite surprising solutions that the rational method might not even conceive.

So the method that I have evolved is a combination of the two. It proceeds in three steps.

First, I use my left-brain, analytical capabilities to try to understand the situation fully. I analyze it thoroughly, model it, discuss it, categorize options, prioritize choices, assign probabilities, ... and then I stop analyzing and go on to the next step.

Second, using my right-brain, I visualize the situation resolved and a decision made. I visualize very clearly what the result will be once I have made the decision. I may pray about it, meditate upon it, do some dreamwork about it, and use other techniques. Then I will release the image of having decided, and I thank God for making it happen. I visualize that the result of my decision has already happened in the present, not the future, and I express gratitude that I have been inspired to make the correct decision or perform the correct actions.

Third, I forget about deciding. I have total confidence that I will be inspired to make the right decision. And I do not worry about it, think about it, or fret about it, for as long as it takes, perhaps some hours or days.

And the inspiration comes. And the decision is obvious. And it is the right one.

So, that method is a balance between the rational and irrational, the scientific and mystical, the outer and inner. I believe that such a balance is valid, and that it acknowledges how we have been created, being part body and part mind/ spirit/soul, part conscious and part unconscious. And mostly, the method seems to work wonderfully well for me.

This method could be titled "Let your intuition be your guide". Your intuition is the most reliable guide that you can have, especially when it is used in conjunction with your analytical abilities, as explained here.

I hope that you will try this method, and adapt it to be a technique that works for you. After all, making good decisions is the basis for using your life responsibly.

Of course, for men there is an easy method. Let a woman decide.

Watching too much television

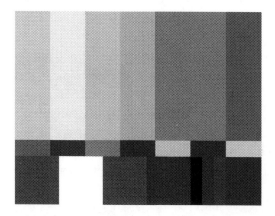

This is a standard North American test pattern for television signals. I think that what should be tested is not the TV signals, but the TV watchers. They need to re-examine how easily they can be seduced into becoming slaves to the tube.

Television is frying our brains and wasting our minds.

To be fair, it is not really television and its electronic infrastructure that is at fault, but the TV programming that is offered to us by the advertisers, networks, and stations.

When our children were just infants, I wanted very much to get rid of our television set. I wanted not to expose the children to the huge amount of crap that was on TV, and to the even larger amount that I predicted would be there in later years.

However, I succumbed. I was overwhelmed by the world's inexorable force, that cultural sucking sensation that made it very difficult to resist having television in the household.

Yes, I couldn't resist. Well, actually, I could if I had really wanted to do so. But I chose a compromise, and did not resist strongly. But I do regret doing so.

Now I fear that society has gone beyond the tipping point. Americans spend more than four hours each day watching television[11]. The same survey reported "The average child will watch 8,000 murders on TV before finishing elementary school"; also that parents spend fewer than four minutes per week in meaningful conversation with their children, but the children spend more than 1600 minutes per week watching television.

Would you believe that there are more television sets in American households than telephones?

Television offers poor quality fare overall, including "reality" shows that are quite blatantly scripted and staged, "Idol" shows that depict amateur singing and dancing as activities worth idolizing, newscasts that offer bite-sized chunks of sensational reports with virtually no analysis, entertainment "journalism" that glorifies celebrities, and an overabundance of murders and violence.

Oh, yes, there is also a small amount of educational programming, cultural shows, and some other good stuff. But those shows are far less attractive and enticing to our tastes than the glamorous junk that inundates the channel selection.

Marshall McLuhan, the famous Canadian communications theorist, called television a "cool" medium, as opposed to movies in theatres as a "hot" medium[12]. Going

---

11 www.csun.edu/science/health/docs/tv&health.html
12 Marshall McLuhan, *Understanding Media: The Extensions of Man*, NY: McGraw-Hill, 1964. See also Marshall McLuhan and Quentin

out to a movie theatre involves you; you have to plan for it, travel there, be on time, and you typically discuss the movie afterwards. You are *involved*, and hot. With television you simply turn it on, sometimes as background noise, you watch whatever is on, you don't need to go out, and so on. You are *detached*, and cool. Watching TV programming involves not thinking for yourself, but being influenced by the "massage". (One of his books is titled *The Medium is the Massage*, and nearly everyone reads that final word as "Message", making the title a wonderful illustration of the power of media to manipulate us by subliminal communication.) Advertising bombards you—and influences you. The clever advertisers and producers create a sense of urgency to keep you watching their seductive shows.

How did we ever let ourselves get in so deep?

Using your life responsibly would suggest resisting the seduction of television programming and regaining the pleasures of thinking for ourselves. Turn it off. Read. Move from cool to hot. Think. Discuss. Live!

Fiore, *The Medium is the Massage* [sic], Bantam Books/Random House, 1967.

Be attentive

This road traffic sign is a warning that something ahead deserves our attention. I view it as instructing drivers to pay attention to paying attention. The upward pointing triangle road sign is standardized to mean warning, or caution. The red border suggests some special importance. The exclamation mark is a standard symbol for emphasis, or alerting us to pay attention.

How many of us really pay close attention to what is going on around us? As Ram Dass teaches, "Be here now!"[13]

If you are anything like me, I would guess that your mind wanders, or you're distracted, and you often do not pay much attention to what you are doing. Even when I am driving a car,

---

13   Ram Dass, *Remember, Be Here Now*, San Cristobal, New Mexico: Lama Foundation, 1971

I'm not fully alert, but my mind seems to be in a sort of "cruise control", occupied with lots of random, fleeting thoughts, while my body goes automatically through the driving motions. It gives me quite a surprise when I jolt awake suddenly and realize how inattentive I had been for the past few minutes of driving!

It takes real effort to be attentive. Being fully aware, alertly present, consciously involved every moment is what I mean by attentive. I have regularly tried to achieve that state, and it does indeed take effort. Life interferes. My mind interferes. My thoughts won't stay quiet; they annoyingly distract my diligent attempts.

But the rewards are great. When I am fully attentive for some minutes, I start perceiving amazing things that I had been unaware of: brilliant colours, sharpened images, subtle music, strange presences, glimpses of other worlds, auras around people, and other perceptions of a larger reality. What I am doing at such times is exercising my under-used faculties, my psychic senses, my mystical insights.

Leaving such faculties undeveloped makes us less than fully human. One way of developing these faculties is by practicing attentiveness.

Here are some exercises you can do to practice attentiveness:

• hold a single thought for as long as you can

• observe the colour green in grass, trees, flowers, and bushes, and marvel at the huge number of textures and shades of green that you can see

- pay attention to the "in betweens", such as the space in between two people, the silence in between two sounds, the time in between two breaths, and the void in between two thoughts

- count very slowly from one to ten and back repeatedly, or from 100 backwards down to 1, not allowing your thoughts to wander between numbers

- concentrate your attention for five minutes on your pituitary gland (or separately, your pineal gland), in the centre of your head, and feel it getting warm

These and other exercises will open up your awareness to whole new dimensions of life that will amaze and delight you. Being attentive reminds me of the Buddhist teaching of Right Mindfulness, one of the ways to end suffering expounded in "The Eightfold Path".

An amusing anecdote about how inattentive I can be has to do with my choice of picture to introduce this article. Without thinking about it, I chose to use two yield signs in this book. The other one introduces the article "Why are gas prices so high?" on page 36. Originally I had used a yellow yield sign for one of the articles, and a red and white one for the other. A reviewer spotted the difference and pointed out the irony of how, in an article titled "Be attentive" I had made the inattentive blunder of using an obsolete image of a 1950s era yellow yield sign. (Now you know my vintage. You also know a bit about my laziness in neglecting to follow my own advice.) Further, my editor spotted another mistake that I had made: warning signs point upwards, not downwards as yield signs do. Sheepishly, I updated the pictures for both articles.

Yes, "Be attentive!" I'm attentive, it would seem, in surrounding myself with good reviewers and editors.

CHAPTER 5: Responsibility to other people

Man's ability to be irresponsible knows no bounds. Creativity in this regard also seems to be unbounded. Here is an example of someone doing maximum damage, creating maximum inconvenience. This cart is not only abandoned, but also blocking a parking spot. This situation is doubly inconvenient. First, somebody else must clean up after the person who abandoned the cart. And, second, every driver that wants to park there cannot do so. Clearly the abandoner felt no responsibility to other people.

Most people see themselves as the centre of the world. That's a valid viewpoint for much of our interaction with the world.

After all, we have our own conceptual views of how the world works.

However, when we interact with other people, we often need to adopt their mental models of how the world works. If we are giving them instructions it is important that we use terminology that is familiar to them. If we are communicating some condition to others, such as a medical diagnosis or a weather prediction, we must avoid the jargon of the medical or meteorological profession. If we make things for use by other people, we should design them for ease of use with minimum requirement for taking training or reading documents.

These considerations involve what is called user-centered thinking. Everyone is a user of someone else's offerings: their products, their instructions, their information, their services, and so on. With that in mind, this chapter gives several examples of how user-centered thinking is the responsible thing to do in our dealing with others.

Setting good examples

Nothing illustrates such a bad example of behaviour as a hockey brawl, a "game" in which "players" are permitted to fight as freely as to "play". And nothing illustrates the degradation of our society as the huge crowds that pay money to attend such games, cheering wildly for the fighting. I call them "hockey workers", not "players", who seem to be permitted, and encouraged, to interrupt their high-paying jobs (not games) with fighting. It reminds us of that other civilization, ancient Rome, that cheered while fighters got consumed by lions, and which soon afterwards collapsed from its own depravity. Will we learn? Or will we continue to set poor examples?

Hockey brawls, obstreperous parliamentarians, neglectful parents . . . All of these, and many more, do a very great disservice for our children.

Archie Bowen, my thesis supervisor, first boss, and later colleague and friend, had an expression about raising children:

> You owe your children three things:
> 1. Example,
> 2. Example, and
> 3. Example!

What a wonderful expression!

I've kept that saying in my consciousness from way back then, when he first told it to me. Years later, I told it to my wife and she loved it, noting that it attuned perfectly with her own belief that what really influences children is the example that you set, not all the preaching and moralizing that you may do.

So, have I taught through example? Have I given my children these three things?

What embarrassing questions! I think it may be best for me just to use my "cop-out" coupon on this one.

I am very aware that I have set a poor example in many aspects of my life as a father. But I know that there were also some good examples, and I'm proud of those ones.

So, using my coupon, I'll just deflect the attention away from me for this one article, and over to you.

How very many opportunities present themselves every day for us to teach by example, not only to our children, but also to friends, neighbours, colleagues, clients, strangers, and, perhaps most importantly, to ourselves! Pick up a discarded candy wrapper. Return your shopping cart (perhaps along with an abandoned one) to the corral. Decline a gift from a supplier. Open the car door, every time, for your partner. Return any excess change that a clerk accidentally gives you. Thank someone for giving a good speech or presentation. Write a letter to the editor advocating your beliefs. Do your job with the highest of integrity. Take the high road. Bite your tongue.

The world is watching your actions. Do they set good examples?

Newton was very clear in his Third Law: Every action has an equal and opposite reaction. That law applies not only to physical systems, but also, as I am sure Newton realized, to social, organizational, psychic, and other non-physical systems. Thus, taking an action that provides a good example sets in motion an "equal and opposite" reaction that we may be quite unaware of. ("Opposite" does not mean resisting or destroying, but simply different or compensatory.) For example, when you return a stranger's shopping cart to a corral, you may influence someone else to return his own cart, or you may plant a seed of responsibility in the mindset of a bystander, or you may cheer up a disgruntled shopping-cart-cleanup worker who is disillusioned by peoples' lack of consideration, or you may cheer up yourself (or an observer) in a subtle way such that later that day you (or the observer) speak kindly to someone, or perform an act of kindness, which, in turn, prompts other acts of kindness, rippling outward, who knows how long or how far?

"Equal?" Newton may have underestimated the magnitude of the reactions from "Example, Example, Example."

See the big picture

It is not obvious that the earth is round, unless you view it in a big picture, such as this one. "The Big Picture" has come to be a metaphor for looking for non-obvious interpretations.

How many of us see the big picture? No, I don't mean seeing the whole earth at a glance, as this picture[14] shows, although that's a good image to keep in mind. What I mean is trying to see things from a perspective beyond that of our own little worlds.

Seeing the big picture means expanding your perspective to include other people's viewpoints. Not doing so often leads to misunderstandings, unintended consequences, and gross mistakes. Doing so often prevents such difficulties by revealing important new information, accommodating the needs of some people that might have been otherwise neglected, and making room for the wisdom of common sense.

---

14   Picture courtesy of the NASA Johnson Space Centre.

It is very easy to get stuck in our own worlds, our own concerns, our own jobs. It often requires effort to see beyond those boundaries.

There are tons of ways that we might not see the big picture. Here are some examples:

- Stopping to see something (in a grocery store aisle, while driving a car, or walking on a sidewalk) and thus blocking traffic behind you. Always look around first before stopping.

- Giving instructions with local jargon or abbreviations. Try to get inside a stranger's head and see how your instructions read.

- Developing software for a PC only, neglecting to generalize it for Macintosh, Unix, mainframes, mobile devices, and other systems. Always follow industry standards, design for generality, and test on other platforms.

- Using relative, not absolute, terminology, such as "turn left", "tomorrow", and "the third exit". Rather, make your terminology absolute, such as "turn Eastwards", "Saturday, August 15", and "The Carling Avenue Westbound exit".

- Answering questions from the audience directly, when speaking to a large group of people. Rather, it is better always to repeat or paraphrase the question aloud so that everyone can understand what the question was, and then to answer it.

You can likely think of many other examples.

The fact that you are reading this book now suggests that you already look for the big picture. Now, get out there and teach others to do so also. Together, we can save the whole big world through seeing beyond our own little worlds.

Always use an editor

Poor, dear door!

This is a picture of a real sign on a real door in a real office building in Ottawa, Canada, where I live. Whenever I see the sign, I chuckle and think, "Oh! Poor, dear door! I would also be nervous and worried after dark, when nobody is around and I am all alone!"

Ha! Isn't that a cute new interpretation? Is it just me, or do a lot of people notice such ambiguous and poorly worded signs?

Building on my work in usability and user-centered design, and my instincts to interpret things literally, I am always on the lookout for such mistakes or ambiguity on signs or instruction manuals.

I see violations everywhere. In Ottawa the main highway crossing the city is Highway 417, and it is known colloquially and locally as "The Queensway". That's fine. But if you are writing instructions for visitors to the city and use something like " ... turn left at the Queensway ... " then your visitor will likely get lost, because virtually no road sign designates the highway by that term; nearly all of them use its official name. An editor would have spotted that error.

Another example is a door sign "Keep doors closed at all times!" which I have seen at a local hospital[15]. How does one get in or out? How very stupid, when interpreted literally! Clearly someone was not thinking clearly. Here's a picture of the doors:

I love "Door" signs and how people don't use an editor while composing them. Here's another that I found in that same hospital:

---

15   The good news here is that, after I pestered the hospital's administration for two years, they decided for their next expansion phase to have a door that has no such sign. Yahoo! Little guy influences big institution once again! Ironically, the sign was redundant, because the doors were self-closing with pneumatic closing devices.

So how are you supposed to leave if you first must lock the door? (Interestingly, some embarrassed staff member wrote in the word "Staff", barely legible, above the top line; that helps, but the sign is still silly.)

Another type of mistake that can be misleading for readers has to do with signs redirecting people to some place to which something has moved. Such signs might look like this:

STORE X

has moved to 123 Main Street

The unfortunate thing about such a sign is that the huge lettering for the store name gives the appearance that this is the actual store, and you have arrived at the right place. But really, the most important text is that the store has moved. An improved sign might be along the following lines:

> **WE HAVE MOVED**
>
> ---
>
> Store X has moved to 123 Main
> Street, three blocks North

Readers of the first sign can be misled to think that the store is still located there; this will frustrate them. Readers of the second sign can tell immediately that something has changed, and they will be alerted to read the whole sign; it is more user-centered. (It also gives two forms of directions: one absolute and the other relative. Such redundancy is often helpful.)

A final example of a poor sign is this road sign on a highway near where I live:

So what do you make of this sign? I think that it is confusing. Should I move over to the left lane? What if I want to go straight ahead? Are only "left turning vehicles" allowed to use the left lane? Or will I find the left lane filled with left-turning vehicles? Or perhaps the left lane is cluttered up with abandoned ("left") turning vehicles. (I admit, that last one is a stretch.) Besides, why have a sign at all? Isn't it always the case that one should move into the left lane in order to turn left?

The key point is one of safety. Drivers of vehicles should never be submitted to surprising situations that may require pondering, second-guessing what a sign means, or irritation. I've never seen such a sign anywhere else. It is not standard, and therefore surprising, and thus potentially dangerous, especially because it is placed at a location where drivers have merged into high-speed traffic. An editor, or indeed anyone applying some common sense, would have spotted the danger here.

I would have argued very strongly to have no sign at all, or perhaps to use a standard sign for "Left turning lane ahead", or possibly—though undesirably—to have worded the sign "Use the left lane to turn left".

A related example is an email message, or a message on a meeting room door, such as "The meeting has moved to Room 123!" Which meeting? Where was it originally going to be? When was it originally scheduled for? Think of your responsibility to other people. Use an editor.

My chief concern here, other than for people's safety, is that sloppy writing is indicative of sloppy thinking. Anyone who designs any document—a report, a sign, a book, or a set of instructions—especially one that might be used by a large number of people, must be vigilant to ensure clear, unambiguous, sensible communication. Not doing so is irresponsible. Doing so is easy … simply recognize that you may be too close to the subject matter to review your own material objectively. Use an editor. Do the right thing: be responsible to other people.

It is vital to take the time and caring to design with the highest of quality. Your creation is your signature.

Note that a professional editor is not necessarily called for. Quite often the job can be done by a critical proofreader, or anyone who is good at being a devil's advocate; in short, anyone who is skilled at adopting other peoples' perspectives.

Think like a user

Great inconvenience, and even disasters, can occur when tools are not designed with real users in mind, workplaces are not designed to handle actual tasks that users perform, and service providers don't think like users. Such situations can include an overwhelming fatigue on the part of workers, increase in error rates, and work flow interruptions.

The simplest, and best, example that I can think of for user-antagonistic (the opposite of user-friendly) thinking is the little compartments for holding batteries in many small electrical and electronic devices, such as flashlights, portable radios, portable CD players, and so on. I hate it when I must insert one battery pointing one way and the other battery pointing the other way.

The reason that most such systems are designed in that manner has to do with connecting batteries "in series". What that means is that the positive terminal of one battery must be connected to the negative terminal of the other one. The total voltage that results is the sum of the voltages of each individual battery.

That arrangement was fine decades ago when portable electrical systems were first designed, and when designers had to build their systems to be very cheap to assemble and manufacture. They put little symbols in the battery compartment to designate the required orientation of each battery. The users had to comply with what the designers wanted. The systems were designed for the convenience of the manufacturer, not the user.

But with modern notions of usability and human factors in mind, it seems obvious to me that a better design for a battery compartment would be to allow both batteries to have the same orientation, and to have a little wire connecting them in the required sequence, that is, "in series". This would be a small inconvenience and a tiny cost increase for the manufacturer, but a great step forward in thinking like a user. For example, Apple's "Mighty Mouse", a wireless computer mouse, uses two AA batteries in it, and they both are inserted with the same orientation. I love it!

Another simple example can be found in elevator user consoles, with their two buttons for opening and closing doors, typically identified by obscure triangular graphic symbols that are hard to interpret, down at waist level or below. Elevator users hate those buttons! But, when you think of it, one button would do the job: a Door button. Pressing it would toggle the current state of the door. If the door is open or opening, pressing the Door button would start it closing; similarly if it is closed or closing, pressing the button would start it opening. Pressing and holding would hold the door in an open or closed state, as appropriate. One button, clearly marked "DOOR"! Further, if it were big and up at eye level, it would be very obvious, as opposed to down in the dark and obscure. Such a design would require a bit of electronics inside the elevator mechanism, and a slight extra cost, but users would love it, because it is so very intuitive in its usage! (Clearly, language issues would need to be addressed; I am only proposing functionality here.) Here's a drawing of my idea for a better elevator console, taken from the cover of my book *Making Products Obvious*:

Finally, a third simple example is that modern user-antagonistic curse, the "insert only in one orientation" point-of-sale payment card reader:

Don't you hate those little devices, with their obscure graphic symbols that you always interpret wrongly, for swiping your payment card? Why do they read the card magnetic stripe only in one orientation? Why should the user conform to the machine, with its limitations, and not vice versa? Shouldn't machines conform to human limitations? Surely a double-orientation reader would not be that much more expensive to make! And how greatly we would appreciate such an innovation! Indeed, it should not be an innovation, but an expected service.

To summarize, users should not have to comply with machine limitations; machines should comply with user limitations.

One of the charming features of human beings is that they make mistakes and they are often afraid of doing so. Machines, which are intended to help human beings perform tasks, should be designed to let their users make mistakes and to recover easily and gracefully from them. It is worth repeating: "Humans should not have to comply with machine limitations; machines should comply with user limitations".

There are lots more similar examples, such as stores that continue to provide multi-queue-multi-server checkout facilities rather than single-queue-multi-server ones; Fax machines that make you insert the paper face down, and consequently you can't read the destination fax number when you need it; and television and entertainment systems with far more complex remote controllers than necessary.

We all can think of situations where we have to stop and think, to second-guess what the system needs, what the designer was thinking of, and how we are expected to use the machine. That's the wrong model. Automation should be expected to serve human users, not the other way around.

Of course, the examples that I have cited here are small ones. Likely nobody will die from poorly designed battery compartments or elevator panels. But when you scale up "Thinking like a user" to large systems, then you can be in the realm of potential disasters. For example, a medical instrument with a confusing control panel might precipitate the dispensing of a wrong dosage of medication. Or a heavy equipment Stop button painted green, rather than the expected red, might trigger a disastrously wrong action in an urgent situation.

So, what I hope that you will do is continually to press for systems that show evidence that their designers think like users. Complain to the managers of organizations that demonstrate systems-centered thinking rather than user-centered thinking. Patronize those organizations that show good behaviour in this regard. Offer suggestions for improvement whenever you see the need.

We can all help to make the world a better place, one user-antagonistic system at a time.

What is clockwise?

Hurricanes form a beautiful spiral pattern when viewed from above. They seem always to turn consistently in one direction in the northern hemisphere, and the other direction in the southern one. But which direction is it?

Did you realize that terms such as clockwise and counter-clockwise are relative, not absolute?

Look at the above beautiful picture of a hurricane spiral. Which way would you say that the spiral is turning? Counter-clockwise, right? Yes, but that's only when viewing the storm from above. When standing on the ground and looking up, the spiral appears to be turning clockwise!

Don't believe me? Then try this little experiment. On a piece of thin paper, draw a semi-circle with an arrowhead illustrating a clockwise turn, as shown here:

Now, lift the paper up and look at the diagram from behind, through the paper. Try it with this very page. What do you see? A semi-circle making a counter-clockwise turn! Yes, it would seem that a turning object must be described differently depending on our vantage point: above or below. Its direction is relative to our location.

And the terms above and below are also relative. On earth, above means away from the centre of the earth, and below means the opposite. But out in space, there is no such reference point. For example, the earth's orbital motion around the sun is often described as counter-clockwise. But that's true only when viewing the earth and sun from "above", whatever that means. From the other side, "below", it would be described as clockwise.

The point of this article is to ask you to be aware of the precision of your communication with others. Which vantage point is the other person using? Is it the same as yours, or different? For precision, you must use absolute terms, or relative ones as long as you specify an unambiguous vantage point.

What sometimes intrigues me is not what we think of the direction in which something is turning, but what that thing itself thinks. What direction does a hurricane think it is turning? What direction does the earth think it is revolving around the sun? If such things could think and perceive, would they have an innate sense of clockwise or counter-clockwise?

What would a clock think, if it had thinking abilities? Would an analog clock think that its hands were rotating clockwise? Visualize the internal mechanism of a clock looking out from "behind" its clock face. By the above argument, it would have to conclude that its hands were rotating counter-clockwise! A similar argument would suggest that a hurricane thinks that it is rotating in the opposite direction than an observer does when looking down from above; and similarly for the earth in its orbit around the sun.

Is there an absolute notion of direction in nature? I would say No, and to illustrate why, let's conduct a small experiment with our own bodies. Please stand up and rotate one full turn clockwise. You very likely would turn in such a direction that your right arm and side moved rotationally backwards and your left arm and side moved forwards. That would be reasonable. Now, if I were on the ceiling looking down on you, I would agree that you had followed my directions correctly. But if I were on the floor looking up at you, I would say that you did not follow my instructions.

And this little experiment assumed that you chose to stand on your feet. Suppose that you had decided to stand on your head. Then everything would be reversed.

So, it would seem that there is no absolute notion of clockwise or counter-clockwise, not only for an observer, but also for the actor.

And keep in mind that the most important view of a weather pattern is not from above, but from below. It is clear why weather patterns are always depicted from above, from high in the sky. We have long been accustomed to geographic maps depicting their domain from above. Weather patterns are simply shown as an overlay on those standard maps. And yet, it is undeniable that the more important view for us is on the ground looking upwards at the wind blowing. So it is very important to consider who is the viewer, or the user, of the information that we provide. What is his vantage point? Which way is he looking?

We need to use great precision, and to be vigilant in adopting others' perspectives—our readers, viewers, and audience—when communicating, if we want to be interpreted unambiguously. Our responsibility to other people includes communicating with precision, so not to allow for misinterpretation.

Don't get me started on left and right, in and out, up and down, and front and back.

VOIP phones and their misusage

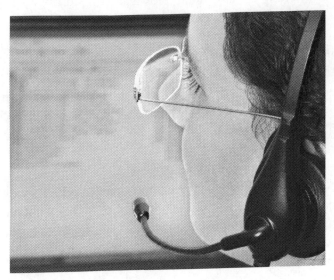

Modern office telephone systems are often integrated with computer systems, so that you make telephone calls with your computer. Many advantages can result, but careful user analysis is needed before implementing them.

Let me tell you about an extreme example of user-centered non-thinking, which illustrates the theme of this chapter marvelously.

A few years ago a major upgrading was done in my city for a local business. A modern, attractive new building was built beside several older buildings, all the employees were moved into it, and the older buildings were demolished. The project received a lot of good press because it was completed ahead of schedule and under budget. Furthermore, a big cost saving was introduced in the operations of the new building: the old telephone system was upgraded to a new VOIP system.

VOIP stands for "Voice over Internet Protocol". It means that the whole telephone system operates in a totally new way, using the modern Internet for its communications mechanism rather than the old-fashioned analog (really old) or digital (modern, but limited) mechanism. A VOIP phone system provides a communications architecture that enables computer communication in addition to voice telephony, and also the potential for integrated applications. A typical example of the latter is when an incoming phone call automatically initiates a customer's account information being immediately displayed on a computer screen for the call recipient to inspect while talking with the caller. That example integrates the calling number delivery feature of the communications system with a database lookup, keyed on the calling phone number.

So everything sounded like good news for this new building. But it was soon discovered that user-centered thinking had not been applied in the design of the communications infrastructure.

The employees found that in order to answer the phone, they had to (1) turn on their computer, if it was not already running, (2) log on to their account, if not already logged in, (3) save their work in progress, in case of a subsequent computer crash, (4) open the VOIP application, if it was not already open, (5) put on their earphone-microphone headset, (6) answer the phone call by using the computer mouse to select the "phone call" icon onscreen, and (7) initiate the conversation by saying some words of greeting. Seven steps, contrasted with the two steps of the old way of simply picking up the phone handset and saying "Hello"! And most of those steps were error-prone due to possible malfunction or system incompatibility. Further, the caller would hear five or six ring tones before a human being answered, contrasted with one or two rings in the good old days. Frequently, the voice mail system would activate after the threshold number of rings was reached and before the call was answered by a real person.

And that's only one scenario. Other horrors occurred when employees found that the Fax machines would not work with the VOIP system, so they had to arrange retro-fitting of old, conventional analog phone lines to the Fax machines. This operation took some weeks, during which Fax communication was impossible. Another horror manifested whenever computer maintenance or upgrading was being done. On several occasions, the computers were out of commission for a couple of hours at a time, and that meant that the phone system was down also. Further, the promised "value added" applications, such as automatic database lookup, were not ready as promised, and eventually their rollout went through incompatibilities and growing pains for the staff. And numerous other user frustrations occurred also.

So, why did all this take place? I would guess that proper planning had not been done. A user needs analysis and life cycle cost analysis would likely have justified implementing a better system initially, in order to make user operations smoother and less expensive in the long run. It sure looked good at the building launch party, but the users, and their clients, suffered greatly later.

What can we learn here? I suggest the importance of our responsibility to other people. This responsibility translates into what is called user performance-centered thinking: design for end user performance, not for system cost minimization.

We can also learn that if your company plans to upgrade to a VOIP system or some such fancy integrated system, then you should make your phone calls now, quickly!

Do the responsible thing: Consider your users, clients, and other such people first, and design for their needs. Design the system so that they are able to perform their jobs competently. Once their usage needs have been accommodated in your design, then plan how to implement the system to meet those needs.

And please note that "design" does not apply only to people working for companies that create products for sale. In everyday life you have the opportunity to design things for others, for example, hosting a dinner party, arranging a family vacation, or remodeling your house. All of these, and many other activities, can benefit greatly from careful design with the needs of end users (your dinner guests, your family on their trip, or the current and future occupants of your house) being of primary importance, and other considerations secondary; in short, by being responsible to other people.

CHAPTER 6: Spiritual responsibility

There is something spiritually poignant about this picture. We see an abandoned shopping cart out in a lonely vista, facing the setting sun, deserted and homeless, bravely and patiently waiting to be put to use again. The winter seems over, with just one snowbank left to melt. A tall lamppost boldly marks the spot, like a flagpole. The distant neighbourhood ignores this bleak scene. The long shadows presage a spiritual death, but the glowing shopping cart, reflecting the sunlight, shines for a rebirth of spiritual responsibility.

First there was spiritual responsibility, and all else followed.

If we lose spiritual responsibility, all else will be lost, too.

This is the most important responsibility of all. Our secular society urges us to compromise our innate sense of spirituality all the time. Many religious institutions teach religion in dogmatic, aloof, hierarchical manners, neglecting spirituality. It takes considerable effort and investment of resources to nurture the inner life, and it can take a long time before results are realized.

By "spiritual" I do not mean "religious". Spirituality does not require membership in a church or worship of a deity. Read on.

Spiritual responsibility

"The Accolade" by Edmond Leighton (1901) represents for me the essence of spiritual responsibility: a young man in ceremonial garb being knighted by an elegant and beautiful young lady. She may be thought of as representing his Anima, the Jungian concept of his spiritual guide and inspiration, the gateway to his soul. He is dedicating his life to her service, promising poverty, chivalry, and obedience. The witnesses (other aspects of himself) authenticate this initiation through their presence and support.

Our biggest responsibility is a spiritual one.

You are not a physical body with a soul dwelling it. You are a soul being dwelling temporarily with a physical body.

This is a very important point. I cannot prove it for you; only you can prove it for yourself. But I can illustrate it.

Consider what your physical body is. It is a collection of chemical elements, configured as molecules, cells, tissues, fluids, bones, and so on. The scientific community generally agrees that every one of the nearly ten thousand trillion trillion atoms in a typical human body, comprising around one hundred trillion cells, gets replaced over the years—often cited as seven years. But at the very least, we know that skin can be scraped off and it regenerates, hair drops out and more grows back in, blood may be lost and it gets replaced, and so on. Yet, through all of this physical change, we still maintain a sense of self; indeed, we know our identity and we know that it persists over the many changes over many years. We are still *ourselves*.

So clearly, we are not our physical bodies. Even if a leg or arm is amputated, we still know that we are the same person. Our memories reach in one continuous sweep back to childhood (and sometimes earlier, to previous incarnations) even though our physical bodies have undergone many changes.

So what are we? If we are not physical, then we must be non-physical. Such a state of being or form can be described as spiritual. We are spiritual beings. Our essence is often referred to as the soul, or the spirit, or the spirit body, or the psychic body, or other such terms. As C. S. Lewis wrote: "You don't have a soul. You *are* a Soul. You have a *body*."

My own preference is the term "soul personality", following the Rosicrucian teachings. I am a soul personality. So are you. So is everyone.

As mentioned, I can't prove any of this for you, but I have proved it for myself to my own level of satisfaction. And you can also prove it to your own level of satisfaction if you really want to do so and are willing to make the considerable effort that is needed. But for the purpose of this chapter, I will accept it as a fact: we are soul personalities temporarily living with physical bodies. I say "with", not "in", because the soul personality not only permeates the body, but also surrounds it. In a sense, the body is in the soul personality.

So, with this in mind, it should be clear that the notion of personal responsibility extends beyond a caring for our mundane physical bodies and environment, to caring for our soul personalities and our spiritual environment. Ordinarily, religious institutions and their associated priesthood have been entrusted with those matters in our society. However, in the same way that our physical matters should not be entrusted to others, such as governments, teachers, or leaders, our spiritual matters should not be entrusted to a religious hierarchy, such as clergy, scriptures, or institutions. As modern, educated, mature persons, we should entrust only ourselves, our inner selves, our inner spiritual guides, with such important responsibilities.

We need to accept personal responsibility for our spiritual welfare. Don't abandon it, as if it were a shopping cart. Study for your spiritual development, research it, honour it, and work on it, to the point that you can detect tangible spiritual growth, new understanding of Truth, and sublime inner contentment.

Reality and actuality

The Sombrero Galaxy, M104[16], is real, but is it actual? A photograph of a galaxy, although real, does not depict actuality. Since the light takes millions of years (about 28 million years for M104), or longer, to reach us, by the time we see it, the galaxy will have changed shape, some of its stars may have exploded, and many other details will have changed its actuality. Also, the light from the far end of the galaxy will have taken significantly longer (about 50,000 years for M104) to reach us than that from the near end, thus distorting the scene and making the image depicted by this picture not actual, but still very real. Finally, the above picture is a time-exposure photograph, far different than we perceive with our naked eyes.

Everything that is real is not necessarily actual.

What is real to me may not be real to you. And what is actual may be different still.

Reality is what we perceive. Actuality is what truly is.

16   Hubble Space Telescope picture courtesy of NASA.

I learned this distinction years ago in my Rosicrucian study, and the lesson has reinforced itself many times as I have looked around and observed the world. The phenomena that I experience are real to me. But they are not necessarily actual.

Take a simple example. I feel hot. The hotness that I feel is real to me. This is my reality at that moment. Right beside me, my wife may feel cold. That is her reality. However, the actual temperature in the room might be 23°C, which is generally considered to be a comfortable value. Actuality is different from reality.

A much richer example is evident in dreaming. What we dream can be very real, sometimes alarmingly so. We can wake up with our hearts pounding, breathing rapidly, convinced of the reality of what we were dreaming. Indeed, it was our reality for a time. Of course, we can then rationalize, after shaking ourselves awake, that it was only a dream. The events that we dreamed were not actual events. The key point is that they were real ones for a time. But, reality in dreams does not necessarily correspond to actuality.

Another very complex example comes from Ufology, the study of unidentified flying objects (UFOs). What can we make of the actuality or reality of such phenomena? Are they actual or real ... in other words are they truly "objects" or just figments of our imagination? I am very impressed by C.G. Jung's book *Flying Saucers*, in which he refuses to conclude anything about the actuality of UFOs due to his lack of full evidence, even after many years of interest. But he does speculate about their reality as a psychological compensatory fulfillment. In short, people *need* to believe in UFOs, and therefore they see them. Writing in 1954, Jung states, "A psychic phenomenon of this kind [a subjective or collective vision, for an individual or a group; i.e., a hallucination—my bracketed words] would, like a rumour, have a compensatory significance, since it would be a spontaneous answer of the unconscious to the present conscious situation, i.e., to fears created by an apparently insoluble political situation which might at any moment lead to a universal catastrophe. At such times men's eyes turn to heaven for help, and marvelous signs appear from on high, of a threatening or reassuring nature."[17]

So UFOs present the possibility of a fundamental difference between reality and actuality.

On an even grander scale, consider the world's many instances of mythology, folklore, fairy tales, creation myths, and sacred literature. They do not document actuality, but reality—or, more precisely, they do document actuality but in a coded, symbolic, mythological, esoteric way. Take just that last example, sacred literature. The Bible has to be one of the greatest hoaxes ever thrust upon an innocent mankind. To consider its stories as actual, rather than real, is misguided. To understand the Bible fully and deeply, one must be a native scholar of Hebrew and Greek, and read in the original languages, so as to appreciate its esoteric and subtle meanings. The Bible, as well as many other mythologies all over the world, presents a vast compendium of universal spiritual truth (or actuality) in the form of stories, allegories, myths, and symbols that primitive people, or the primitive aspects of evolved people, can relate to (i.e., their reality). The mistake is to confuse reality with actuality.

And that's the main point that I am trying to make here. If you can hold that distinction (reality *vs.* actuality) clear as you contrast your own world view with what actually exists,

17 C.G.Jung, *Flying Saucers: A Modern Myth of Things Seen in the Skies* (translated by R.F.C.Hull), New York: MJF Books, 1978, p. 131.

then such a model will help you understand and evolve toward Truth. And Truth is what you want to know in order to focus on the responsibilities that you have: personal, civic, and spiritual.

Reality is one's Truth. Actuality is *The* Truth!

The most important thing

*The magnificent displays of brilliant Northern Lights (*Aurora Borealis*) evokes a sense of awe and wonderment, inspiring us to wonder what is out there, where are we in the cosmos, and what is bigger than us.*

What is the most important matter that mankind faces?

That question was asked of me in a random telephone survey some time ago. I thought for a brief time, and asked, "You want my honest opinion?" On getting an affirmative answer, I asked further, "And do you want the truth?" At this point, the pollster likely felt like dropping the call, or perhaps marking it "No opinion," but we continued.

I chose my words carefully. "The most important matter facing modern mankind is the loss of a sense of the Divine!"

The momentary pause at the other end of the line perhaps denoted a search for the category "Other," and the pollster then politely thanked me and ended the call.

I still believe what I said then. Most people would perhaps cite global starvation and poverty, the AIDS epidemic, global warming, the worldwide economic crisis, or the threat of nuclear war. Some people would note terrorism or the runaway population increase. Still others might note man's inhumanity to man or the threat of an asteroid bashing into the earth. But I maintain that our loss of a Divine sense is our most important, pressing matter.

Now, by this I don't mean to argue for membership in a temple or mosque, or "going to church", or adhering to the dogmas of an organized religion. What I do mean is the sense of wonderment and awe when faced with anything apart from common everyday experience. I mean the numinous feeling of contemplating creation and its ongoing evolution. I mean the quickening feeling of experiencing real silence within, and exploring its profound and vast depth. I mean the thrilling attunement with the cosmos that comes from sudden realization that *you are the cosmos*. I mean having a religious and mystical sense that comes from within, not from external dogma. I mean truly realizing the enormity of the unconscious, and that great energy and truth can be found there.

Having a sense of the Divine gives life a purpose. Having a sense of the Divine motivates us to a higher morality than that of animals who go through life by instinct alone. Having a sense of the Divine assures us that we are not alone.

Man's inhumanity to man can be traced to a loss of the sense of the Divine. Indeed, all of the calamities that I listed earlier, and many others, can be traced to a loss of a sense of the Divine (possibly even the asteroid).

So can we recover? Is there hope? Is the half-full glass emptying or filling?

Carl Jung wrote about an American Indian tribe that prayed to the sun each day, persuading it to rise every day, and thus giving them a purpose in life. That was their religion, their sense of the Divine. They must do their daily ritual. If they stopped, mankind would perish.

Jung also wrote, "Among all my patients in the second half of life … there has not been one whose problem in the last resort was not that of finding a religious outlook on life. … This of course has nothing whatever to do with a particular creed or membership of a church."[18]

I must hope that the glass is filling, that we will recover, that there is indeed hope! That is my religion: contributing to mankind's creative evolution through my own recovery of a sense of the Divine. Perhaps one such contribution might be a reminder to my readers that having a sense of the Divine is a wonderful way to enhance one's level of personal responsibility. This is because seeing our world through divine eyes gives us the biggest picture of all, thereby making us aware of our responsibility to be proper stewards of our world and our lives.

---

18 C.G.Jung, *Modern Man in Search of a Soul*, New York: Harcourt Brace Jovanovich, 1933

Develop your conception of God

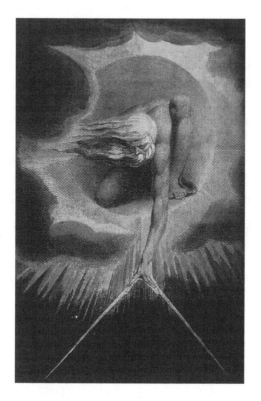

William Blake's beautiful painting God As An Architect *(1794) stirs my emotions as I consider the Grand Scheme that God had in mind when creating the universe, even though it wrongly conveys an anthropomorphic image of God. Mythologically, it is valid, but not literally.*

What is your conception of God?

I don't mean what the clergy or religious leaders teach you, or what your parents told you, or what the Bible or other sacred literature says. I mean what do you believe in your own, inward self?

It's an important question. God is what makes the universe tick, what gave you life, and what sustains your life. So it is vital that you have some conception of what God is.

I can't tell you what to believe. But I can give you what I think is correct, as a model and example for you to consider.

This article documents not the absolute truth, or actuality, about God, but my conception, or my reality, of God. I would love to know the Truth, the actuality of God, but that may take longer to achieve than I have available even in this lifetime. And my conception will likely evolve in the future, as it has in the past.

First, God exists. God is. God is God. It is divine, pantheistic, and everywhere.

Next, what is God not? God is not a wizened, bearded, old man dwelling in Heaven, pulling the strings of the universe. God is not masculine only. God is not the jealous, capricious YHWH of the Old Testament. God is not Zeus or Jupiter or Thor or Allah or The Father, or any of the popular conceptions of most of the organized religions.

So what is God? I think that *God is Nature*. God is the collected Laws of Nature. When I conceived of this definition a few years ago, I felt very relieved, as a whole structure of Truth seemed to fall into place.

The Laws of physical nature are well established, or at least many of them are. Newton's laws of motion, Kepler's law of planetary dynamics, Faraday's laws of electromagnetism, Einstein's laws of relativity, various laws of Biology, Chemistry, Anthropology, Psychology, Geology, and other disciplines collectively encapsulate our knowledge of the physical universe. But there are also laws of non-physical nature, that is, mystical and spiritual laws, such as the law of the triangle, the law of karma, laws of psychic projection and healing, and many others. Collectively, all of these laws, physical and non-physical, comprise God. I use the term (capital N) Nature to refer to the totality of physical and spiritual nature.

God is impersonal. The laws of Nature apply equally to everyone without exception. God does not know my name, nor treat me any differently than anyone else. I can choose to ignore the laws of Nature, or to cooperate with them and to apply them to improve my life. Prayer does not change God's mind. It applies its laws impersonally. Prayer does work, but for different reasons than is often thought. The petitioner uses words to make his appeal, but unconsciously he attunes his spirit to the object of his prayer and to God, thereby using the Law of the Triangle quite unawares. That channel, which enables God's healing love to flow through the petitioner to the object, is what makes prayer work. How very much more effective is prayer when the process is done consciously, not unconsciously!

God is not exclusively masculine, but rather all genders: he/she/it. My own preference, in keeping with Nature-equivalence, is to refer to God as neutral: it.

Further, God is pantheistic. This means that God is distributed throughout the Nature that it created. It is not external to that Nature, but part of it.

God does not perform miracles. A miracle is the temporary and localized suspension of the laws of Nature. Such things simply do not happen. Even in or near a black hole Nature's laws hold. God is constant. Through studying Nature and developing one's capabilities, one can direct Nature to cause manifestations, using laws of Alchemy, that might appear miraculous, but that are entirely consistent with the laws of Nature. We just may not understand them all yet.

We are created in the image of God—the spiritual image. (There is no physical image.) Spiritually, God is part of every one of us. We are aware of its influence on us through our inner self. The self in turn uses our conscience, emotions, and intuition to deliver to us messages from God. Further, our spiritual bodies extend far beyond our physical bodies, and they can influence events that may have personal meaning for us, events that we might classify as chance or coincidence. We have complete free will to ignore or to listen to any of these various messages, that is, we can work against or with God in our lives as we see fit.

As above, so below. That expression originated with the medieval alchemists and the earlier Hermeticists to capture their view of spiritual truth—God—being mirrored on the physical plane—Man. The dynamics of the spiritual plane, which can be abstracted as God, are indeed reflected and duplicated in the dynamics of the physical plane, abstracted as Man. This view might partly explain why the early Egyptians modeled their spiritual pantheon on human images, which mythology was later refined by the Greeks and Romans.

As within, so without. That is the other half of the above expression in Hermetic philosophy. It comes from the notion that God is accessible from (some would say identical with) our inner selves. With this in mind, listening attentively to our inner self (through meditation, dreamwork, recognizing our intuition, and so forth) can be considered listening to God's voice speaking to us.

So why do so many people believe that God is a wizened, old, bearded man sitting in Heaven, capriciously dispensing favours and punishment? Fear of the unknown, I would guess. Power of the priesthood might also be a contributor. Also, man is by nature gregarious, and enjoys belonging to groups and sharing beliefs with others. And, perhaps most of all, it could be man's timidly absolving himself of responsibility for his own life, and turning over his affairs to a stern parent figure who can be appeased or angered, and can comfort or punish, on a whim. That model was valid for primitive mankind, but is quite inappropriate for modern, thinking, aware adults. I think that it is long past the proper time for mankind to grow up, to think, and to be open to other possibilities.

Furthermore, if God really did look physically like us human beings, how would the many beings on the vast number of other planets feel about that? It is highly unlikely that they all look like us: arms, eyes, legs, and so on. But their view of God would very likely evolve to an image that looks like them. So, therefore, God must not look physically like us. Spiritually, yes, but not physically. Indeed, God is pure spirit, or pure mind.

But our anthropomorphic view of God attests to the power of Myth. Sophisticated mythologies have evolved in all cultures to explain matters of the spiritual plane. Those mythologies have become a reality for those various cultures. But the actuality of the universe is far different. The mistake that has been made by so many people in their unfortunate absolving of responsibility is to confuse reality with actuality.

The view of God as equivalent to Nature might help mankind to evolve to the next level of spiritual maturity.

My hope is that your own development of a conception of God will similarly help mankind to evolve to the next level of spiritual maturity. You have a vitally important responsibility, a task to which you can contribute uniquely and with great effect.

Prayer works!

There are many forms and definitions of prayer, spread through all organized religions. A great many people believe in the power of prayer. But very little teaching is done in how to pray with true effectiveness.

Prayer works, but for a different reason than most of us believe.

Yes, it does work. But not optimally.

Most people would define prayer as appealing to a deity for some intervention, such as healing a sick person. Many of us believe what our religious institutions taught us, and what we learned as children. Pray to God or Allah or some deity for a specific person or cause, and He will grant your wish. Such prayer can be made more effective, for example, as the Christian church teaches, if we invoke the intervention of an intermediary such as Jesus Christ, who is reported to have claimed that any prayers directed through him will be fulfilled. Other intermediaries can be the Virgin Mary, various saints, and so on.

By these conventional means, our prayers request that a miracle be performed, such as curing a sickness, or assuring the success of a venture, or enabling a hockey team to win a game. As described earlier, a miracle is the spontaneous, temporary, and localized suspension of the laws of nature. Thus, by means of a miracle, the biological laws of nature are to be overturned momentarily so that the sick person recovers; the law of gravity or strength of materials or whatever is to be suspended for a specific venture so that it succeeds against all odds; and the Toronto Maple Leafs, against all analytical predictions, win their championship match. Most other sick people die, many other ventures fail, and other teams lose to the Leafs, all because they were not prayed for.

Do you see how irrational it is to pray for a miracle? Miracles simply don't happen. The laws of Nature persist unerringly and impersonally, and they will not change because someone prays for them to change.

And yet, such miracles do seem to happen. What's going on here?

Effective prayer involves recognizing that God is the impersonal energy underlying—or equivalent to—Nature, and to direct that energy through yourself to the object of your prayer. It is not God that does the healing or that influences a venture to be successful or that makes a team win its game. It is *you* who accomplishes those things, with the assistance of the natural energies of the universe.

This concept is elaborated in "How to pray", the next article.

How to pray

There are many ways to pray. This picture might be helpful in suggesting alternatives to a conventional Christian form, by combining it with a Yoga-style meditative posture.

Prayer is a mystical process, not an intellectual one.

The way we have been taught to pray by clergy or other religious leaders is to make petitions to God in the form of "Dear God: Please make Jane better," as an intercession when Jane is sick. That method is wrong. If God is omniscient, as the same clergy teach us, then surely it already knows that Jane is sick. Why does God need reminding from us? Such a model would suggest that God is teasing us, being petulant, or even cruel, by knowing that Jane is sick and doing nothing about it until we remind it of the fact and beg it to correct the situation. And how do we explain the case when Jane does not recover, but gets sicker, or even dies? Do we then blame God for ignoring our pleas? Do we explain the outcome by admitting that it was

God's will? Do we carry on, praying in the same ineffective way as before, gambling on the outcome? Or do we do the intelligent thing and observe the failed experiment, examine the premises of our prayer model, develop a new model, test it, and eventually find a model that works better?

A much more effective method of prayer involves recognizing that it is a mystical process, meaning that it involves direct union between yourself and God. First, be aware that the only person whom you can really change is yourself. Therefore, your prayer should be that God guides you to be the very best person that you can be. In the case of sick Jane, your prayer should be that you be guided to be your very best in helping to make Jane better. Don't expect a miracle. Don't expect God to do the work. Expect yourself to do the work.

Second, how can you do effective healing if Jane is a long distance away from you? This step involves realizing that she is not a long distance away. She is connected to you. We are all one. There is only one soul in the universe, the Soul of God. We are all part of that Soul; indeed, we *are* that Soul. We are all One. So Jane and you are the same. You have different soul personalities, which have incarnated into different physical bodies. But the essence of you and the essence of Jane are the same.

So contacting Jane does not involve a long trip to touch her physically. You are always in contact at the fundamental level, the level of the soul. Thus, being your very best for her is something that you can do at the soul level. And you can make a tangible contribution to her life, in terms of healing, inspiration, and encouragement.

Third, we need to realize what sickness is. Sickness is an imbalance of natural conditions in a person. Healing involves rebalancing to a state of harmony. This model applies also to organizations, institutions, countries, civilizations, and even the world, any of which may be sick. They can all be treated by rebalancing their natural conditions.

Fourth, we need to examine the mechanism of how you can have an impact on someone using the mystical Law of the Triangle. Two points, properly focused, will manifest a third point for stability. The first point is the sick person, Jane, for example. The second point is God. You can visualize the connection among Jane, yourself, and God, and feel God's healing love flowing through you to Jane. Then the third point of the triangle, Jane's healing, is made manifest. The process of God's love flowing through you awakens the natural healing energies that are latent in Jane, bringing about a balanced, harmonious condition for her.

Fifth, if Jane is receptive to the above process, it will be much more effective than otherwise. So coaching her in advance to want to get better, to make herself receptive to healing energies, and to let her know that you will be an instrument of healing for her, is an important part of the overall process. Receptiveness is also improved by having her examine her life to remove any blockages to health, such as poor eating habits, smoking, drinking alcohol, or holding negative thoughts. She should switch to positive thinking and adopt healthier habits, such as meditating, eating good food, drinking lots of clean water, and exploring the topic of mystical healing. But assure her that the real healing comes from God, and that you are merely an instrument, or a channel for that healing energy.

Sixth, finish your healing session by thanking God for using you in this way, and then dismiss all thoughts and worries of Jane, and adopt a sincere attitude of total confidence that

Jane's health has improved. The process should be repeated daily, or more often, until the desired results are evident.

Now, that's effective prayer. I learned it from the Rosicrucian teachings, as the "Rosicrucian Art of Absent Healing", and adapted it to my own style. It involves work on my part, not simply petitioning God and then expecting God to perform a miracle. And it is a suitable method not only for healing sicknesses, but also for any situation that you want to affect: a safe trip for someone, guidance for proper choice of a mate, wisdom in decision making, and so on. Such considerations lead to the seventh requirement: your motivation for prayer should be non-selfish, altruistic, and in noble fulfillment of your responsibility to continue co-creating the world along with God. This form of prayer will likely not be effective in helping your favourite team to win, or for you to have "good luck" in a lottery, or to make it not rain on your picnic, unless, of course, you can formulate your wish to comply with a higher, non-selfish purpose, such as sharing your winnings with a charity.

We're not finished yet. The eighth requirement is that you actively show your gratitude for your answered prayers by giving back something of yourself from the benefit that you have gained. For example, make a donation to the hospital where your friend was treated, write a letter of thanks to a doctor or a politician or a police department or whoever helped the situation for which you prayed, or at the very least put some money into a private holding place for later anonymous donation to a charity.

So prayer involves extensive work on your part, not just abandoning your spiritual responsibility by asking God to do the work. What a shame it is that our spiritual institutions continue to mislead us by teaching that prayer is easy, and that God changes its mind in response to prayer!

I encourage you to think seriously about the effectiveness of your current form of prayer. You are an evolved, mature person who can think for yourself. Consider prayer a form of scientific experiment: formulate a model of prayer; use it; test it; observe results; form conclusions; modify the process or develop a new model as appropriate; test that model; observe results; and continue to evolve new models until you are satisfied with the effectiveness of your prayer model.

If my explanation here is helpful in evolving your own prayer model, then I am pleased that I am able to help. Indeed, as you might guess, I have been praying, using my process, to be my very best for you, my fellow human beings, and I am totally confident and grateful that I have been helpful.

Why are the pews so empty?

All that beauty of hand-crafted wooden pews, with stained glass windows, ornate art, and centuries of beautiful music, all going to waste.

Now that I have advocated a higher-level view of God, approached with a mystical and awakened attitude, I want to return to my own religion, Christianity.

I am a Christian … but not in the conventional, orthodox sense. My quest is to understand what Jesus really meant in his teachings, what the Bible really means in its writings, and what God is really trying to tell me through my inner self, and then to follow that guidance. I believe that Jesus, who became The Christ, was the very best, most valid, of all our spiritual teachers, and I hope that mankind can evolve to the point of truly understanding, and living, the actual, esoteric, fundamental teachings of Jesus.

In short, I want to understand Truth, or actuality, not simply truth, or a reality as promoted by the organized religious teachings of the Christian church. The church teaches truth in the form of a mythology; Jesus gave us Truth in the form of symbolic, esoteric, mystical teachings. My quest is to understand, and follow, the latter teachings.

With this in mind, I offer the following dialogue in the hope of stimulating the evolution that, to my way of thinking, is needed.

———————

Why are the pews so empty?

Because people are not being nourished in Church.

What would nourish them?

Spiritual food. People need to be taught about spiritual food, how to find it, how to choose the good food, how to consume it, and how to digest it. Such teaching is not being done in the modern Church.

What should be taught?

Mysticism. This means direct union with God.

What is being taught instead?

Religion. This is an indirect union with God.

What's the difference?

In a religion, one has faith in the revelation of someone else, usually the founder or teacher of that religion. One gets information from scriptures of the religion, and one follows instructions and guidance of the priests and teachers of that religion.

With mysticism, one has one's own revelations directly from God, not indirectly through someone else, or through writings or instructions of others.

Are you saying that the Church practices religion and not mysticism?

Yes.

Is that why the pews are so empty?

Yes.

Can the Church teach mysticism?

Yes, by liberating the church leaders to teach the people to practice mystical exercises, and to grow in Christian mystical spirituality.

What's wrong with the traditional teachings?

They were appropriate for a less evolved people, with their stories and simple images and threats of consequences. But people have evolved, and they need more advanced teachings to help them to evolve still further. The Bible is taught as if it were literal and historical, when it actually should be interpreted symbolically and mythologically. Worshipping a remote and unattainable Jesus is not what is important, but awakening and nurturing the Christ within us.

Isn't mysticism anti-Christian?

Jesus was a mystic. He was not a Christian, but a Jew. He practiced a form of Jewish mysticism. He would likely be very unhappy with today's Church and how it has misrepresented and distorted his original teachings.

Can you give me an example?

> *Yes. In John 14:12 (RSV), Jesus declares, "... he who believes in me will also do the works that I do; and greater works than these will he do ..." But the Church does not teach us how to do "the works". Rather, it has robes and rubrics, rote recitation of prayers and petitions, and praising of Jesus. Jesus never asked to be praised. And he never asked to have a church founded in his name. He always taught of "The Father's" glory, not his own.*

What will happen if the Church does not change, to teach mysticism?

> *Pews will be even emptier. People want to embrace spirituality. If the Church will not give it to them, they will seek it elsewhere.*

Where will they find it?

> *Some will look to other religions. But the true seekers will explore various organizations for mystical and spiritual teachings. These include New Age groups; mystical and initiatic orders; study groups in mythology, symbolism, and esoteric knowledge; spiritual Alchemy and the Kabbalah; Martinism, Freemasonry, and Rosicrucianism; and various others.*

Where can I find such groups?

> *Ask your priest or clergy. If he will not tell you or help you find a suitable group, he will soon be out of a job. The pews will be totally empty. Lots of groups will come forward to fill the void. Then you can easily find one.*

But let us hope that your priest will indeed help you, rather than hold you back in your spiritual quest. If your priest has your real interest at heart, then he will help you truly to evolve, and in so doing, help the church evolve.

Is there hope for the Church?

Yes, of course there is. The Church is headed by God; therefore it cannot fail. What will facilitate its success is for mankind to listen attentively for God's guidance for its Church, and courageously to follow that guidance. Besides, it isn't the Church for which we should seek hope, but for mankind. And, yes, there is great hope for mankind. People are evolving. The Church can help or hinder their evolution. The hope lies in helping.

Live by the golden rule

Friends treat each other well. They want to be treated the same way.

The Golden Rule states "Do onto others as you would have them do unto you", and all sorts of variations of that, such as "Do not do to others as you would not have them do to you" (sometimes called the Silver Rule). Its philosophical name is the Ethics of Reciprocity. Virtually all the religions of the world have some version of the Golden Rule at the heart of their teachings. For example, in Hinduism it is stated as "This is the sum of duty: do not do to others what would cause pain if done to you", in Islam it is "None of you [truly] believes until he wishes for his brother what he wishes for himself", and in Judaism it is "What is hateful to you, do not to your fellow man. This is the law: all the rest is commentary". Confucianism has a nice version: Tse-kung asked, "Is there one word that can serve as a principle of conduct for life?" Confucius replied, "It is the word 'shu' — reciprocity. Do not impose on others what you yourself do not desire." And there are many other variations, all with a similar intent. It is arguably the most important rule ever formulated for mankind's guidance.

So why is the Golden Rule so seldom respected and followed? We all can think of many instances of it being "more honoured in the breach than the observance", to adapt Hamlet's pithy observation. Each of us could cite wars, lawbreaking, fighting, political backstabbing, cheating, breaking one's promise, misusing our world's resources, neglecting the underprivileged, and many other examples. Why is this the case?

There are likely a great many explanations for such behaviour. My own favourite explanation is that we can ignore the Golden Rule because we have learned over many generations that there are quite often *no immediate consequences for ignoring it*. Through repeated experiences, we have learned that there are often no consequences for offences such as parking illegally, for exceeding the speed limit, for petty stealing, for polluting the environment, for supporting or participating in wars, for abusing our family members, for breaking marriage vows, or for cheating in business transactions.

However, there are certainly some long term consequences. Ignoring the Golden Rule adds negatively to our karma. (The Law of Karma governs the positive and negative compensation we receive for our actions.) We will experience some compensation later in our current life, or in some future one.

But the long term is far away. The short term is what counts for most people. It is easy to fool oneself into thinking that the only real things, the only things that matter, are those that are perceived by our five physical senses. If one does not immediately feel the pain of breaking the Golden Rule, then things are OK. Carry on breaking.

Thinking, responsible human beings should make every effort to understand the Golden Rule and to apply it diligently in their daily lives.

Even shopping carts should be treated with the Golden Rule. Indeed, all of the topics in this book should be approached with the Golden Rule in mind:

- Shopping carts: Don't abandon them, because you would not want to be abandoned.

- The earth's environment: Don't abandon it, because you would not want it to abandon you.

- Society: Don't neglect your civic responsibility, because you will want society to treat you well.

- Your life: Use your life responsibly, and it will reward you greatly.

- Other people: Take good care of your family, friends, and clients, and they will take good care of you.

- The spiritual world: Be the very best spiritual being that you can be, and you will prosper and evolve optimally, in this life and in subsequent ones.

Postlude: A conversation - 2

"So, do you think that it worked?"

Zenoch pondered before responding. Even though he was an optimist and viewed the glass as half full, he knew that the important matter was whether the glass was filling or emptying, and perhaps the rate of filling or emptying.

"Well ... " he offered, hesitating to make a firm pronouncement. "It would seem, at least on the surface, that humanity's descent may have slowed down, and perhaps even turned around."

Netherfeld teased him, part jokingly, and part seriously, "Oh, come on! You, the optimist, being upbraided by me, the realist! Of course it has turned around! Just look at any measure that you like. Fewer wars. Quality of people's eating habits has increased. Melting of the icecaps has nearly stopped. What more do you want?"

"Yes, those measures look good. But they are merely the superficial indicators. The really important thing for long-term sustainability is whether humanity has grown spiritually. Have they captured a sense of a greater reason than themselves to take care of the world? Have they regained a sense of the Divine?"

There was still a great deal of uncertainty about human beings and their earth. With more than seven billion people and a planet under great strain, one could never say for sure that the future would be smooth. Anything could go wrong: a gigantic earthquake, a deadly pandemic, a terrorist madman starting a new global war, a collision with a huge asteroid, an invasion by an alien predator, worldwide economic collapse leading to massive famine, or any of several other natural processes that could destroy the delicate equilibrium that was developing on earth.

There was no cause for Zenoch and Netherfeld to relax or to take a break from the constancy of their sending good thoughts to their charges on that tiny, delicately balanced planet. One day they also would be incarnated in human form again, as needed for their own development, and as needed for humanity's evolution. Until then, and thereafter, their work was greatly needed.

But they could still wonder, and chat, and learn.

"You know, a really neat thing is how Bezanson responded to our psychic signals to him. He wrote a book about saving humanity and the world, and you and I appear in the book. Isn't that neat?"

Netherfeld was skeptical. "Yes, I know. But my question is how he knew about us, and how did he know our names? And that in turn leads to the even bigger question of which came first, him or us? Did we inspire him to write a book with us in it, or did he create our 'earth contingent' through his imagination and spiritual alchemy, perhaps in response to some other psychic inspiration that he had earlier received?"

"Fascinating! All good questions." Zenoch responded. "I would guess that they all can be answered by one statement: I think that Nature made it all happen, following natural processes. A long time ago, more than sixty of their years, Bezanson's soul personality was sent to that specific body in anticipation of a great need. Of all the possible parents, locations, and timeframes that could have been chosen, Nature arranged for him to be born to them, there, and then. Nature knew that the world would be degenerating due to overpopulation, pollution, global warming, and mankind's self-centered greed and aggressiveness. So Nature arranged for many people to have a mission of saving humanity and the world. Bezanson was one of them.

"So which came first, him or us?" he continued. "Well, it would appear that we came concurrently. Nature needed all of us. You and I to support and inspire Bezanson and others, and they to respond to our inspirations.

"And his book appears to have been widely accepted and read by an enormous number of people. They have matured and taken responsibility for their own lives. And we, Ahem!, can take pride in the fact that we inspired most of those people to want to read the book, and to tell others.

"Not that pride was our motivation, but a desire to see creation evolve. And, of course, we must acknowledge that higher-level soul personalities have been guiding us."

Netherfeld was caught up in the excitement of how everything was connected. "And our own support network kept us on track, right?"

"Yes, that's right."

"But how can Nature be so smart as to anticipate several decades in advance just what would happen and what sort of action would be needed?"

Zenoch had meditated on that question many times during his earthly incarnations and also while on the spirit plane. "Well," he mused, "When you think about the fact that there is no such thing as time or space, and, even though we lower-level beings have a hard time understanding such a counter-intuitive concept, Nature has no trouble at all in understanding and using it. So seeing several decades into the future is not difficult at all for very advanced adepts, the most advanced of which is Nature itself! Seeing into the "future" is simply done by seeing into a different aspect of the present, like a different dimension. And, if we follow Nature's guidance, we all are the beneficiaries."

"Wow! Even I am becoming more and more impressed by the enormity and oneness of natural processes! I, who have been so fortunate as to evolve to quite an advanced level, can still be astonished by how magnificently it all works together! Even I can catch a glimpse of how much farther I have to evolve, and how much more there is to learn!"

Zenoch and Netherfeld looked out and saw that it was good.

The realist would come to understand that the glass is half-full.

The optimist would come to understand that it is gradually filling.

Appendix: Further reading

There are many readings that are appropriate if you wish to explore some of the topics that were introduced in this book. I suggest the following:

For environmental issues, and our responsibility to working towards a sustainable environment, I recommend the Earth Future web site: www.earthfuture.com. Its organizer, Guy Dauncey, is very prolific in this area, and many references and links are available on that web site.

For spirituality, and our responsibility to our spiritual selves, I recommend the EnlightenNext web site: www.enlightennext.org. It contains references to courses, books, and other relevant materials. Especially relevant are the writings of Ken Wilber, accessible from that site.

For reading more about the Rosicrucian Order, there are several such orders, and I recommend the one to which I belong, the Confraternity of the Rose Cross, described on its web site: www.crcsite.org. It contains links to related orders and publications that may be of interest. Information can also be requested by mail to Confraternity of the Rose Cross, PO Box 304, Tillson, NY 12486-0304, USA.

If you like to look at pictures of abandoned shopping carts, try feeding "Abandoned shopping carts" into a WWW search engine. Much of the material will be of the eCommerce nature, but there are a couple of really good web sites that you will find about physically abandoned shopping carts in Toronto and Los Angeles. There is even a great sounding book on the topic, *The Stray Shopping Carts of Eastern North America: A Guide to Field Identification*, (although I have not read it) available at www.amazon.com/Stray-Shopping-Carts-Eastern-America/dp/0810955202.

To read further about our responsibility to other people, specifically on the subject of user-centered design, I recommend my own books *Performance Support Solutions: Achieving Business Goals Through Enabling User Performance*, available from amazon.com or from the publisher at www.trafford.com/Bookstore/BookDetail.aspx?BookId=SKU-000148787, and *Making Products Obvious: Performance-Centered Design*, available from the publisher at www.baico.ca/html/store/shop/index.cfm and searching for "Bezanson". My own interest in this area is in what I term performance-centered design, which involves designing things in ways that allow the performance of users to be measured (such as error rates, task completion times, and amount of training needed), thereby reducing life-cycle costs by designing to make users more effective in their jobs.